# CANADIAN GINGER

# CANADIAN GINGER

edited by

Kim Clark & Dawn Marie Kresan

OOLICHAN BOOKS

FERNIE, BRITISH COLUMBIA, CANADA
2017

Library and Archives Canada Cataloguing in Publication


Canadian ginger : an anthology of poetry & prose by and about redheads

/ Kim Clark, Dawn Marie Kresan, editors.


Includes index.

ISBN 978-0-88982-322-8 (softcover)


1. Redheads--Literary collections.  2. Canadian literature (English)--

21st century.  I. Clark, Kim, 1954-, editor  II. Kresan, Dawn Marie, 1974-,

editor


PS8237.R44C36 2017          C810.8'03561          C2017-906956-X



We gratefully acknowledge the financial support of the Canada Council for the Arts, the British Columbia Arts Council through the BC Ministry of Tourism, Culture, and the Arts, and the Government of Canada through the Book Publishing Industry Development Program, for our publishing activities.

Published by
Oolichan Books
P.O. Box 2278
Fernie, British Columbia
Canada V0B 1M0

www.oolichan.com

# CONTENTS

| | | |
|---|---|---|
| Kim Clarke | ix | Preface |
| Dawn Marie Kresen | x | Introductory Note |

## GINGER ROOT

| | | |
|---|---|---|
| Winona Linn | 15 | High School Biology |
| Bruce Meyer | 16 | Delaney |
| Heather Spears | 19 | You Have the Reddest Hair I've Ever Seen |
| Diane Tucker | 21 | Freckles |
| Tracy Hamon | 22 | Permanent Colour |
| Christine Lowther | 24 | Shades of Red Through Time |
| Kim Goldberg | 28 | Heather Mead |

## GINGER FLAME

| | | |
|---|---|---|
| Bruce Meyer | 31 | I Glow |
| Aidan Chafe | 32 | Diary of a Redhead |
| David Fraser | 33 | Strawberry BlondE |
| Penn Kemp | 35 | Ginger Reflections |
| Heather Spears | 37 | I Want to Run Barefoot Through Your Hair |
| Tracy Hamon | 39 | There Once was a Red-Haired Girl |
| Kateri Lanthier | 41 | My Red Hair |
| Jennifer Zilm | 42 | Two Postcards from a Redhead in the Desert |

## GINGER SNAP

| | | |
|---|---|---|
| Rebecca Păpucaru | 47 | For the Daughters of Chernobyl |
| Charlie Petch | 48 | #48 Copper Red |
| Margaret Atwood | 50 | 'Nobody ever did want me' |
| Diane Tucker | 58 | Tiny Dresses |
| Jordan Watkins | 60 | Double Recessive |
| Winona Linn | 63 | Red Fox |
| Joanne Levy | 64 | Seeing Red |
| Jennifer Zilm | 68 | West Coast Letter to My Ginger Twin |

# GINGER SPICE

| | | |
|---|---|---|
| Anita Dolman | 73 | Calico |
| Carolyn Clink | 75 | Supper with the Sphinx |
| Maureen Foss | 76 | Thistle |
| Lizzie Violet | 78 | Foxglove |
| Rachael Preston | 80 | Once a Redhead |
| Carla Hartsfield | 84 | You and My Hair |
| Margaret Atwood | 85 | Hairball |
| Darryl Whetter | 98 | The Extinction |
| Heather Haley | 100 | Winter Heat |
| | 103 | Editors |
| | 104 | Contributors |
| | 112 | Acknowledgements |

# PREFACE
BY KIM CLARK

You know that flash of inspiration you get for a project, that bright tiny inkling that you just know will be fun and fascinating and worthwhile—seeing a particular type of diversity from the inside rather than the standard alternative with its associated myths and histories. Seeing it through a wide variety of voices.

I had that flash, a title—Canadian Ginger—but nothing more. A year went by, then another. Sure, I'd been busy, but the inkling persisted with frequent redhead reminders both in person and in my newsfeed. The idea gradually grew but I wasn't prepared to go it alone. Before I approached a publisher, I needed to find another editor—someone whose literary work I admired who'd be willing to share their time, enthusiasm and, yes, the work. (It was so difficult to choose!) I needed that person to be Canadian and to be part of the less than 2% of the population with red hair. I found the fabulous Dawn Kresan who had all those attributes. But this is confession time.

Dawn and I are part of an even smaller group, less than 1% of the population, and this is what sealed the deal. We both have MS, the abbreviation for multiple sclerosis and for manuscript. Kind of cool and weird, no?

I think so. Cool and unusual like this project, that took off with the help of Oolichan Books and a choice array of natural and temporary Canadian Ginger authors.

Massive thank-yous to everyone involved!

P.S. Have you heard the one about the twenty-seven redheads walking into a Canadian book?

# INTRODUCTORY NOTE

BY DAWN MARIE KRESAN

Does the carpet match the drapes? The first time I was asked this I was fourteen, standing on a diving board, about to jump into a heavily chlorinated pool at the Holiday Inn. Two boys stood on the edge laughing. I ignored their question and dove into the cool water. It wasn't until I had front-crawled the length of the pool, climbed the ladder and begun drying my hair, that I realized what they were going on about. I was mortified. The heat spread through my body like wild fire, in a full-body flush that fevers over the surface of the skin. It's impossible for a redhead to hide embarrassment.

Fast forward twenty-five years. I'm on vacation, soaking in the near scalding water of the resort's hot tub, when a drunken man informed me that I was exceedingly sunburnt and suggested that soaking in a Jacuzzi was a bad idea. I assured him that I wasn't sunburnt and he, in turn, assured me that I was wrong. The woman across from me weighed in. She was a nurse and explained that natural redheads were more prone to vasodilation when overheated. He turned to look at me, boorishly eying me with a new-found appreciation. "Oh, I didn't realize you were a natural ginger. So, I gotta' ask, does the carpet match the drapes?"

I realized early on that gingerness was a physical trait open to public discussion. My red hair was a beacon signaling strangers, inviting conversation, whether I wanted it or not. I have friends who are both naturally blonde and boxed-hair blonde, and both groups tell me their hair doesn't incite this type of curiosity. Like a woman wearing lipstick—sometimes it's obvious and sometimes not, but in either case, it's of little concern to other people. For some reason though, perhaps due to its inborn rarity, being a ginger demands explanation. "Who'd you get your red hair from?" I don't know, I'm adopted. "Do you ever tan, like… even with a base?" There's no such thing as a base with redheads. We just burn. "Do you always have sunscreen on?" Yes. "Do your freckles fade in winter?" No. "Is it true redheads feel less pain?" Dunno. "Redheads don't have blue eyes!" Um, sorry? "Wasn't your hair redder before?" Blonde is a ginger's grey. I'm fading as I age. "Are you a genuine redhead?" I'm not sure what you're asking. "Does the carpet match the drapes?" Fuck you.

As a child my hair was vibrant copper, but as a teenager and a woman in my twenties, it was strawberry blonde. I read that hair texture and colour changes every seven years. It can become straighter, curlier, darker, lighter, or more brittle, due to an influx of hormones in puberty or an underactive thyroid in middle age. Essentially, our hair follicles are at the mercy of our ever-changing body chemistry. And then there is the damage we willingly inflict on our scalps. While in university, when money allowed, I'd lighten my hair to a flaxen gold. My roommate would watch me mixing a concoction of pigments and processing agents, and say in a disapproving tone, "please stop wrecking your hair." The next day she'd lecture me with a slow shake of her head, "women pay good money to have their hair look like yours." Then it happened. In my thirties, my hair naturally began to lighten. I learned to appreciate it just at the time it began to change. An ironic reversal. A ginger Greek tragedy.

I met Kim Clark several years ago, at a reading for my newly released poetry collection, coincidently about another redhead, Elisabeth Siddal. We stayed in touch afterward, and a couple years ago she asked me if I wanted to be involved with an idea she had for an anthology. As she proceeded to tell me about *Canadian Ginger*, my mind shuffled through snapshots of memory. I'd never really considered it before, but "redheadedness" did have its own history, tropes, misconceptions and stereotypes. I need look no further than my husband who, in one of our rare but intensified arguments or debates, will throw his hands up in resignation and say, "well, I did marry a redhead," as if that's all the clarification needed.

If I could quickly run through a list of experiences, initiated by nothing more than my hair colour, then other redheads would have similar stories— perhaps funnier, or more salacious, or more brutal. I hadn't previously thought about it, but now that I was, I could see Kim was onto something. Yes, we gingers have stories that are uniquely ours. This anthology showcases a number of them.

# GINGER ROOT

## HIGH SCHOOL BIOLOGY

Punnett squares explain
dominant and recessive traits
simple evolution
and the colour of flowering peas.

But Punnett squares don't explain
how this hair and skin
decided to settle in this body
in this family
in this genetic line
or what colour of red seeped through.

Is it Hudson's Bay point blanket red,
bitten tongue red,
raw meat red,
Red Earth red?

Is it blood-on-the-dirt red?
Burning villages red?
Or is it just Irish red, *other side* red, embarrassed whispers red.

Punnett squares explain
the possible combinations of maternal and paternal alleles
but they don't answer my grandmother
when she asks *what colour is this*
as she tugs my side-braids
at every family reunion.

## DELANEY

When his mother cleared her house, he remembered how red his hair had been.

The barber draped a white chasuble around him, gave him a paper collar like a minister, and fastened both at the back of his neck with a clip. His hair was bright ringlets, that had always been part of him; but as they fell he began to cry.

His mother hushed him. "Sit still and let Mr. Delaney do his work." Snip, snip, followed by the buzzing razor up the back of his neck.

"There," said Mr. Delaney, "smooth as a kitten's wrist."

That next night his mother moved him out of his crib into a big-boy bed. He lay awake, sobbing softly so no one would hear. He was not crying for the yellow crib and its bars, but for the red curls Mr. Delaney swept up and threw away.

At the supermarket, his mother pushed him in the cart's seat. Other children pointed and laughed. At the checkout, he climbed aboard the mechanical pony, a palomino, with a black-stirrupped saddle and reins that ran to the horse's mouth. His mother promised she would buy him a ride when she finished. An older fat boy came along and pushed him off. "Get off of there, Red," he hollered.

He had gone out to the garden to play soldier. His aunt had given him a navy blue, toy Civil War cap and said, "There, General," then saluted. He shot at bad guys from behind trees, but most of the time he lay down in the grass, wounded.

He woke crying that night. His mother wrapped his arms with Ozonol and gauze. "Because you are badly sun burned." He walked around for three days wearing the Union hat and pretending he was a wounded soldier. He imagined people asking him how it happened and he would answer, "during a charge."

When his mother took the bandages off just before his nap, he screamed. There were brown spots all over his arms. There should not be brown spots on his arm. He begged his mother to take them off.

"It was the Ozonol," he cried.

His mother shook her head. "No, no, they're just freckles because you have red hair. They are also appearing on your face because you were in the sun too long."

He stood on his dresser and stared in his bedroom mirror. He had wounds on his face. The freckles looked like brown bugs. These bad things were happening because the barber had cut his hair.

When his favourite hockey player, Red Kelly, was signing autographs at the hardware store, he had been pushed to the back of the line, and instead of waiting longer, he walked away. Kelly never looked up. People were always pushing him. No one pushed hockey players, not even ones with red hair.

His grandmother had taught Sunday school. He felt very awkward the few times he went. He felt badly that Jesus died. It was his fault. The picture at the front of the Sunday school room was of a bearded man who appeared to have red hair, but that was because the picture had been in the sun too long. One of the girls teased him when sunlight caught the brush on the back of his head and she ran her hand over it. She said it reminded her of the cat her sister had shaved.

His grandmother caught him running through the house one day and said, "You are becoming a heathen." She gave him a book she had read as a child, *Hurlbut's Story of the Bible*. The pictures were colourful. Adam and Eve were crying behind some bushes as an angel held a bright red sword. A group of men were trying to pull a stone block attached to some ropes.

He brought the book to his mother. A tall red-haired man was standing between two pillars, his face contorted to a grimace.

"That's Samson, the strongest man in the Bible," she said. "He disliked his enemies so he pulled down the pillars of the temple and crushed them all. A woman called Delilah cut Samson's hair and he thought he had lost all his strength because everyone said his strength was in his hair." The temple pillars were curly-cue like the pole outside Mr. Delaney's barber shop. He devised a plan.

Early one morning before anyone was up, he got dressed and left the house on his tricycle. He brought a length of rope his father had left in the garage. Mounted either side of the shop door were two wooden posts with red, white and blue stripes twisted around them like snakes. He stood on the rear platform of his tricycle, wove the rope around the poles, and then wrapped the remaining two ends around his handle bars. He climbed aboard and began to peddle his trike as fast as he could. He climbed aboard and peddled his trike away from the doorway as fast as he could. He felt the jerk, heard a snapping sound behind him.

He saw one of the posts coming away from the doorframe, so he reversed to get a better run at it, and revved up again. His tricycle snapped backwards beneath him and he went flying to the pavement. The loose pole came away from its moorings and struck his head. He dreamed that a cat with short hair, red in the sunlight, was licking his face and giving him more freckles as he lay on the sidewalk. He dreamed his head was being shaved. He felt weak.

When he opened the envelope that contained some of his mother's keepsakes, he found a curl of red hair.

"Was I really that red when I was a kid?" he asked her, as they sat eating lunch surrounded by boxes.

"I saved that from your first hair cut. Mr. Delaney cut it very short. I think it shocked you. You cried. You said you hated him. You were a wild child. We never knew what you would do. You were always cutting your head open, playing Superman, or falling off your trike. Too much energy and imagination and too little to do. That's when the doctor said we had to put you on skates, and is probably the reason you play hockey now. I chalked it up to the red hair. Sometimes we never knew why you did things, like that incident with Delaney's poles. Whatever possessed you?"

"I remember that. I thought I was Samson. Delaney, Delilah. I was one confused kid." He tucked the envelope with its curl in his shirt pocket.

"Well, Samson, after lunch I need you to take those boxes to curb for the junk man. They're full of metal that your father hoarded. They weigh a ton. I can't lift them."

"No, problem," he said, taking the final bite of his sandwich, and got on with his work. He still hadn't shaved off his playoff beard. Sunlight reflected into his eyes off the long red strands. He picked up the first box, then the second, and figured he could carry at least the third the length of the driveway. The more he piled one on the other, the stronger he knew he was.

## YOU HAVE THE REDDEST HAIR I'VE EVER SEEN

Once Auntie took me to tea on a houseboat
under the Georgia Viaduct by Stanley Park.
I was 8, nothing was explained, I went along with it
the man a church acquaintance possibly.
Moo, neat in her office clothes,
pearls, brimmed black hat
the cramped, canted cabin
tea, knick-knacks on chains
and then him going on and on
with a stupid urgency about my hair
how I must look after it, never forget
to brush it every day,
all my life take very special care.
A grownup, a stranger saying things to kids
that they don't care about or understand.
Maybe he touched my head, big deal, I can't remember.
If Moo cut our visit short I can't remember.

Mother did my braids each morning
(3 me's in the mirrors at her dressing table)
she pulled so tight it hurt.
Bored in school, I chewed at the end of a pigtail
—the ironish taste,
tough skiddery wires between my teeth.

Mother wouldn't let us dance
or sing for the sightseers
Saturdays in the open streetcar labouring up Dunbar
when kids performed from the sidewalks
and got pennies thrown at them.
Or enter the freckle contest either.

Nabokov said we had "silverfish eyelashes."
I tried to get mine dyed, saw a furtive ad in the *Province*:
*"With lashes fair, you'll get no dare*
*Tinted, they'll take you anywhere."*
Downtown, upstairs on Seymour Street,
I had to sign something in case it went wrong.
I said I wanted brown.
They came out jet black.
I tried to powder them.
As they grew in—zebra striped.
The white eyelashes of the true redhead
the sallow skin
the white eyebrows.

DIANE TUCKER

## FRECKLES

I am a fat bud
of melanoma waiting to bloom.

I watch every brown spot, waiting for it
to lose cohesion, darken, sprout
a mottled twin or a brand-new beard.
The doctor is used to me
flashing him the latest one.
"Age," he replies warmly.
"It's an age spot."

This is better? Death is death.
Maybe time is slower than cancer,
but both those trains pull into
the same station in the end, dear doc.

Whenever the telltale mark appears,
or if it never does, each spot is a day,
a month, a year the skin has spent and shed.
They are time's paw prints, the little beast,
measuring me for my grave. They are the body's
dress wearing thin. Darkness showing through.

No cancer yet. But even these spots,
the ones they called, so sweetly, "freckles"
can hardly bear the happy name "benign."

TRACY HAMON

## PERMANENT COLOUR

MC1R is a recessive gene
on the 16th chromosome of the human—

two of which are needed to create
hair the shade that can be called red

auburn, orange, cherry, scarlet, ruby
cerise, ginger, carroty, garnet,

claret, burgundy or crimson.
Bottled and applied, it's more popular

than blonde or chestnut, though the fun
factor is unconfirmed.

Who was it said, we fear most
that which we desire?

How did we learn
to single out our differences?

Maybe contemporary ideals can diagnose
history's didactic symptoms, can explain why

a ginger-haired man was hunted
in an alley by an apothecary's thugs

because those were the dark ages
and the fat from a red-headed man

rounded out the perfect poison
needed to rid the world of those

less desirable. Or why Lilith,
fashioned from the same dust

as Adam was different
by thinking we're all equal.

Or why head hunters during the inquisition,
plucked women with green eyes and freckles

for trial, then tied them
to the stake of what we forget.

All this fear passed forward
as legends and hieroglyphics

by people who couldn't make up their minds
whether hair colour was lucky

as the Irish or cursed like Judas. Only four per cent
of the people carry this gene, but the others are afraid.

CHRISTINE LOWTHER

## SHADES OF RED THROUGH TIME

"I get a lot of support from people in the ginger community."
~Rupert Grint

By chance, riffling through some old files the other day, I came across a class picture: 1977–78, grade five. Big collars, polyester, stripes and patterns on the clothing of the children and the teacher. One of the girls in the front row stretches her smile to show both rows of teeth. She wears an off-white blouse with a few flowers around the neckline, plus a naff little orange bow. Her skin is paler than anyone else's. Her sneakered feet pose neatly together, hands are clasped, head slightly cocked. She looks like bully bait. She's the class's only redhead. She is me.

Was. Two years later puberty struck, and God painted my head brown. I say God, because that's how hard I had been praying for it. The red was merely my cotyledon after all. What a relief! It was adults—classmates' parents, my grandmother—who admired red hair. Not other children. The popular kids were usually blond. In an era known for its tanning obsession, we were pale, often plump. And the freckles! My face looked like the aftermath of a fart through a rusty pipe.

> "I have not got spattergroit!"
> "But the unsightly blemishes upon your visage, young master—"
> "They're freckles!" said Ron furiously.
> ~J.K. Rowling

In my world, every physical attribute of a redhead was unattractive and unacceptable, despite *Gilligan's Island*'s Ginger. To gain any sort of popularity one must put in hours of effort, and the only tool left was personality. Exhausting. It felt impossible to hunker down and lick one's wounds when one's head was aflame. I couldn't cover my pain and hide. It's shocking to me now, the level of self-hatred at such a young age. And it never went away, until 1991 when I read Naomi Wolf's *The Beauty Myth*. Something every person should read. Annually. By the time I was ready to stand up, stand out, veer off the mainstream, make a statement, only my freckles gave me away.

Entering the punk scene in my mid-teens offered new modes of expression through hair shape and colour—blue, black, green, orange, purple and scarlet. I tried them all, often several at once. I started noticing men who were naturally ginger. I even settled down with a redhead in my twenties and thirties, accepting my natural brown head or adding only henna to it. But a punk can't be put down. Eventually I bleached my hair and added "extra-red" henna. The result was bright. I know now that I was attempting an emphatic reconnection to the child I had been.

Maybe it was more than my hair colour that got me bullied; maybe it was the flood pants and the ringlets, the name Christie (which I changed), my big mouth or the fact that kids just like bullying. Back then, there was zero adult consciousness about it, no "It Gets Better" campaign, none of this progressive kindness. Plenty of kids were terrorized. One of the nastiest kids, in fact, was a ginger named Gary. As soon as it was safe enough, well into adulthood, I accepted the notion of seeking what I'd lost: memories of the parents who were both gone before I was eight years old, answers to a thousand questions. Taking back childlike pleasures such as tree climbing and roller-skating.

I began to talk to other gingers randomly. In a bus line-up, at the library, at work. "What do you make of being a ginger?" One young man claimed that Canmore, Alberta had a high population of gingers when he was getting his education: a whole school bus full. I assumed he had not, therefore, been bullied?

His smile faltered. "Yeah, I was bullied a little. I mean, we stick out like a sore thumb."

And now?

"I do get annoyed when people I don't even know call me feisty."

Another one came into the gallery where I work, no doubt thinking she could quietly browse the local art in peace. "How do you like being a ginger?" I asked her.

As a child, she went to school in Barrhead, Alberta, while living in the nearby town of Whitehead, travelling to class on the Yellowhead highway. Her classmates had a saying about her. "The Barrhead redhead from Whitehead via Yellowhead gives good head."

I sometimes get the feeling that everyone admires red hair but would never want to have it. On the HBO series, *True Blood*, red-topped Arlene was angry at her boss for hiring a second red-haired server at Merlotte's Bar & Grill because redheads always got the best tips. But who was the main character of the whole series? A blonde. Buffy the Vampire Slayer was blonde, too, whose best friend and side-kick, Willow, was the redhead. And the same again in *Xena*. The Warrior Princess was a brunette; her side-kick was Gabrielle, who had light ginger hair.

I know. I sound petty. The girl in the class photo looks, of all things, supremely happy. How is it possible? Was it the wholesome, Canadian influence of *Anne of Green Gables*? Hardly. As Wikipedia puts it, Anne was "pathologically insecure about the colour of her hair." The Swedish Pippi Longstocking was my girl. Pippi was a proud redhead, impervious, strong, and completely confident, with no parents in sight. A child who lived alone with her pets, she was my heroine. In real life, it must be said, girls have little defence against the onslaught of popular culture. I was too young to enjoy or appreciate being red, too hurt to shrug off a "sore thumb." Statement-making came later, once the hair was naturally (and commonly) brown. Without parents, there was already too much "sticking out," and all of it weighted with shame. Life had so far been kind of crazy. Continuing on as a carrot-top might have killed me.

The red hair was part of the worst time of my life, but only part. I wish I could reconcile with that nerdy, pale, over-smiling kid. I never had children and I'm not confident around them. If I see a kid with red hair, I make lavish with the praise, just like the grownups did with me. But I also make a point of adding, "I'll bet you're a clever sort" or "Why, look at the intelligence in those eyes!"

I've continued questioning other adults I don't know. Recently, outside the ferry terminal, I approached a white-skinned, freckle-faced redheaded man and blurted, "Can I tell you something you already know? You've got great hair." And I've been telling them about this book. Writing about gingers is good for us.

A true redhead, Rupert Grint, played Ron Weasley in the Harry Potter films. He was thankful to author J.K. Rowling (past redhead, present blonde). "Do you know what you've done for gingers?!" he once said to her. He spoke of something we have that people of other hair colours perhaps don't—community. We benefit from each other's support, and accept, appreciate, admire and celebrate one another. Our skin might glow in the dark. Our freckles might look like spattergroit. We true Goths might need to hide from the sun. Canada can be a cold place, yet sunscreen is definitely required. In the end, all will be in the past and I must embrace the grey.

Sources:

http://www.rupertgrint.net/rupert-grint-quotes
*Harry Potter and the Order of the Phoenix* by JK Rowling
https://en.wikipedia.org/wiki/Anne_of_Green_Gables

KIM GOLDBERG

## HEATHER MEAD

In the highlands of Scotland, beside a loch
not found on any map or known to even the wildest
backwoodsman, live the last surviving
Neanderthals on the planet. The three youngest
females have come of a certain age. They spend
long hours grooming each other's strawberry
manes, shooting green-eyed glances
at their muscular cousins while rubbing their own ample buttocks
against the scrabbly bark of pines along the shore.
The elders begin to worry. They furrow their generous
brows, huddle and mumble in the caves at night.
They may not know or care that their genome
has been mapped or that their nucleotides have leapt
the species barrier or that Scotland has the highest
percentage of redheads in the world. But deep
in their creative brains, endowed as they are with a superior
visual cortex, they can see the diminishing returns
if their young beauties have no suitors beyond their kin.
And so a plan is concocted along with another batch
of Heather Mead (care being taken to preserve the powdery
fungus on the underside of the leaves).

Three elders set out across the highlands, travelling
by night, keeping to the trees until they spy
a flock of sheep. A young shepherd slumbers on the heath—
his skin as pale as the full moon above, hair as bright as
rowan berries. Years later, all he will remember is a strange
dream where he lay staring at paintings on a cave ceiling,
flames dancing and leaping from a pit, his porcelain skin
slick with sweat as three fiery goddesses spread themselves
on top of him, one after the next.

# GINGER FLAME

BRUCE MEYER

## I GLOW

My mother never let me wear red.
I dreamed of firetrucks, bright balloons,
the crimson serge of marching bands.

She insisted red was not my colour,
said I would appear to be on fire,
a bright lick from a candle's top.

But after a brilliant summer sunset
when the campfire wore to embers,
I whistled gently on an orange clunker

and recognized my hair in radiance.
That night I slept, praying that dawn
would rage like a sky I forged inside.

AIDAN CHAFE

## DIARY OF A REDHEAD

Mother called me Aidan.
Father called me son.
Ireland called me Little Fire.
In kindergarten, they called me Freckle Face.
Third grade, Carrot Top.
Ninth grade, Fire Crotch.
On the sporting fields, Fiery.
At the ocean-side summer camp, Lobster Boy.
Around the neighbourhood, parents knew me hot-tempered.
On the beach, blinding.
In snow, camouflage.
In mythology, they called me Thor.
After death, they thought me vampire.
In cinema, wild and tangled.
Once, after posting a fresh-haircut profile picture online,
a college friend messaged me, said I reminded her of Tintin.
On Robson Street, they called me Daniel.
On Granville, they called me Henrik.
In England, they called me Rooney.
In China, Red Devil (Gang Mo).
In Australia, they garnished me Ginger.

You,
You call me Beautiful.
Beautiful.
Beautiful.
Beautiful,
the way you repeat it
until the word

extinguishes everything.

DAVID FRASER

## STRAWBERRY BLONDE

Hey, we ain't goin' away, baby,
'cause our genes are everywhere,
not just on the surface—even that third of you
with the black, going-on-grey hair got the gene,
the flame-hair gene, the ginger gene.
That's ginger with a long 'i' as they say in Scotland, bro'.
So get used to it, we're here to stay.

Some say we're natural born killers
if you believe the history.
Napoleon, Oliver Cromwell and Custer
had red hair, but maybe they just made that up
to support their fears.

Well, I'm strawberry blonde,
not the orangutan carrot-tops like my cousins.
Too, too red. Even I am prejudiced.

See, I'm strawberry blonde, not red.
but if I grow a beard, I'm ginger.

I won't tell you about the does-he
or doesn't-he girls in college
who dyed their hair to match mine,
secretly wanted to get into my pants
to see if I was authentic.

I won't tell you about the bullies,
all the punch-ups at school.
Thought it was because I was short, had an accent,

not my hair.
It's not easy for a guy who's red and thinks he's blond.

Even strangers knew my name.
*How ya doin', Red,* they'd say.
But I'm Blond, Strawberry Blond.

And when I was young, older women in my life would say,
*"Such a shame. He should have been a girl."*

PENN KEMP

## GINGER REFLECTIONS

As a girl nicknamed Copper Penny, I was not allowed to wear red, orange, pink or purple. Those colours—convention, and my mother, told me—would clash with my hair. So I was dressed in blues and greens, and the occasional yellow. As an adult, I have delighted in wild colour, though my strawberry blonde ringlets have now faded to a non-descript ash.

Being born with red hair places you as an outsider, a small minority that is singled-out as both odd and special. As a youngster, to meet redheads in fiction was to look into a curious, distorting mirror. The reflection was not necessarily true to form, but it offered possibilities, a myriad of reflections to my wondering ten-year-old eye.

The redheaded girl in books was invariably curious, intriguing, and intrepid. She was a sharp-nosed detective like Nancy Drew, determined and resolute, if insufferably righteous. She was a rebel like Pippi Longstocking, the strongest girl in the world, who didn't mind being unusual and lived independently in her very own house. She was the quintessential Anne Shirley, whose impulsive courage and outspokenness were admired and imitated. I identified with these wild redheads of fiction, from comics, crime fiction, through to Victorian novels. These flaming beauties had strength of mind I respected, though their persevering conviction frequently got them into of trouble. My own wilfulness was similarly blamed on my hair.

Beyond the pale, out of the ordinary, the redhead is the fiery other. The dangerous Siren, the one who tempts. The one who burned. She is Rider Haggard's Ayesha, with her masses of red hair. She is Circe, Lilith, Boadicea, Mary Queen of Scots, always the outsider, but queen of her own domain. The redhead is witch or, as Elizabeth 1, she is royalty. She is myth and archetype, always willing to stretch the limit, to risk her own head. The redhead is as dangerous as she is endangered.

In movies, television shows, comics and cartoons, she is Batwoman, Jessica Rabbit of *Who Framed Roger Rabbit* and Wilma Flintstone of *The Flintstones*. She is Gillian Anderson as the fearless Dana Scully in *The X Files* and the luminous Julianne Moore in *The End of the Affair*. She is Joan Holloway in *Mad Men* and Willow Rosenberg in *Buffy the Vampire Slayer*. She consistently goes against the grain. She often finds herself in grave predicaments, from which she usually, but not always, escapes. It is the redhead who dies betrayed and betraying in Mickey Spillane's crime fiction.

For male artists, she might be Mystery, Anima, the unknowable: a projection of the unattainable. Dante Gabriel Rossetti elevates the lustrous, copper-haired Elizabeth Siddal to become his beloved Muse. But because she is beyond the human, she is doomed as Millais' newly drowned "Ophelia" or Rossetti's angelic "Beata Beatrix." And on the opposite end of the spectrum is the red haired female poet, who saw her hair as a symbol or power. In Sylvia Plath's "Lady Lazarus," she ominously chants, "Out of the ash/ I rise with my red hair/ And I eat men like air."

I embrace my red headedness. I am the wild one, the one who kicks aside convention and heads off into the woods on her own. The one whose face still freckles and burns. The Irish one, the Scot, the Celt. When I see another redhead, I see a kind of errant sisterhood. I look at her and think, *aha, another mischief maker. Let's play!*

# I WANT TO RUN BAREFOOT THROUGH YOUR HAIR

At UBC I wore a ponytail tied with a black
velvet ribbon. Sitting in on Honours English,
a sudden tweak—whispers, students behind me
conspired to pull out a hair.
I was shy, though I must have startled,
wouldn't turn around.
That was the class where Dr. Daniels asked
about the *Ode to Joy* and everyone was impressed
when I said "Beethoven's *Ninth*"—
but I'd listened to it the first time ever
(records from the library) the night before.
Everything I excelled in
was a kind of fake like that.

When I was anorexic my hair fell out
no one knew that word, or what was wrong with me
the doctor I was sent to
said I had "*too many male hormones*"
whatever that meant
which was why my periods had stopped
and pointed out lanugo, long fair down
on my languid arms.
He gave me pills I never took.
I was 16, no one had figured out
what I was doing. So I quit trying.
Ate. My hair grew in again.

Grace knit me a Fair Isle sweater
green on white. In the kitchen on 34th
I'd lean back over a boiling pan

before a party, to wave my hair,
singed the sweater and got in trouble.
Worked in mental hospitals in the summers—
my Weyburn prairie hair was straight,
humid Toronto at Queen Street, curly.
The dorm girls liked to make
a hairdo of it. I let them.
No one admired the colour—at best outrageous.

What I remember, my life's thread, as it was.
Now in old age faded, sad, bald, pink.

TRACY HAMON

# THERE ONCE WAS A RED-HAIRED GIRL

She was a barber. He was a man
of a certain age wearing an expensive suit
black leather shoes buffed to shine
polished as silver, his shirt
a soft blue cotton, tiny-patterned
paisley tie. He stepped forward
as if from legend, once heroic
jawline slumped by time
and mourning. His eyes carried
defeat from finding his best clothes
in the closet his wife had kept free
of dust and moths that devour woolen
elbows and underarms. He wants her
the red-haired woman in a shop of men
to cut his hair. And when it's his turn
he lowers himself down, places
fingers on the chair's arms
as she turns him to face away
from her and the mirror.
The cape's nylon wall
makes it easy for him to tell her
his story, the comb's teeth sliding under
wounds, each word a lightening
that suspends his wife mid-air
amid electricity's soundtrack
conversation's echo in the busy shop.
His wet cheeks are neither performance
nor catharsis but a casualty of loss. She
lingers on the last touches, letting others wait

while sweeping every hair
from his forehead and nose
removing the small paper
sheet from around his neck.

## MY RED HAIR

Was it '70s film stock that first lit the flare?
Light-haired baby, auburn kid. Now I choose my red hair.

Small-screen siren comedienne, curled-lip long-stemmed rose.
Unbeliever! Fingers fire-walk through my red hair.

Spray-painted for raves: silver nitrate, cyan, lime,
washed next day to ruby embers. Trash is treasure, my red hair.

Bookish kid, owlish adult. Did Lucy Maud miss *her* "e"?
Anne could burn down Green Gables with my red hair.

Postpartum red-handed, bleeding for what's gone and here.
Pale blue newborn eyes focus on my red hair.

Pin-ups: Garnet, Ruby, Beryl. Sardonic wise-crack Sardonyx.
Lust's objective correlative: my red hair.

Phoenix. Firebird. Plath. I will eat them like air.
Set your mouth near my temple. Fire-breathe my red hair.

Red Kat, October poet, you're no immortal Red Tārā.
The fire in snow, the flash in opal: my red hair.

Jennifer Zilm

## TWO POSTCARDS FROM A REDHEAD IN THE DESERT

1.rainbow over Masada

Now I see how the sand is manuscript: the desert                    unfurling
upward and all around us—a scroll. My sun-punctuated body
calligraphy scaling the snake path. At four am: a flat tire—Sharif pulled
the *sherut* into the road's shoulder—and we waited
until a trucker hauling Maccabee beer stopped to provide assistance. I heard
them
speaking Hebrew too fast for me to catch the words. Anyway, we missed
the sunrise and now I am hiking the hill in sandals,
trying to conjure the A/C in my Hebrew classroom
and how Rikvi—our Kibbutz raised, philosophy
trained *morah*—tried to convey the density of the Hebrew verb:
"*every time I say* '**I speak**' *the letters hold both* '**word**'
*and* '**desert**'—*the wilderness where G-d spoke*
*and disclosed to us his name.*" And the desert is speaking
my ginger skin bright, bright red. Buzzards circling my dizzying
head: my dense, dense freckles.

1.Qumran: the scriptorium and the mikvaot

The Hebrew word for red is *adom*. But this is dirt,
not skin, hair. At the Frank Sinatra Student Centre cafeteria
yesterday a cook took one look at me and said *ma ratzah, gingy?*
My vocab is limited but I know *what* and *want*
so I pointed to couscous, sweet & sour chicken, said *zot*
[this]. Nevertheless, conjugate me.
I redden among these underwhelming ruins,
a lonely red planet gingerly being led by Sharif
to a phrase deciphered from papyrus, plastered

on the wall by the Antiquities Authority, in Hebrew
and in English: "*they shall eat together and bless together, and take counsel
together.*" Sharif tells me that 'take counsel' means 'to console.'
The aspirant waited a year before reaching to touch the shared bread,
for two years to tip a simple clay cup of unfermented red
wine into his mouth. The word for community is *yahad*,
which—if you play around with vowels—could mean either *one*
or *together.* The real miracle, as always is irrigation
A complex of networks to harness the winter
rains for *mikvaot*—that stagnant water could still purify.
There is nothing on the wall to tell me but I guess
bathing was a solo journey. I imagine my body,
sun punctuated, walking the steps down into one of these cisterns,
the hot damp swallowing bare skin, a desert Ophelia, a surfacing
rush of red hair.

# GINGER SNAP

Rebecca Păpucaru

## FOR THE DAUGHTERS OF CHERNOBYL

*Start at the roots*, you said, reading
the box like a manual. I shook the plastic
bottle until the fumes made my eyes
water. I soldiered on, following orders,
prodding my scalp with the plastic nipple.
I had nothing to lose but the everyday
auburn that bored you.

You preferred exotic girls,
not Molly Ringwald meets Dora Maar,
but some alt-porn star from the Ukraine,
the girl in *My Girl Friend's in a Coma*.

Because I could, or not, because the choice
was mine alone, I closed my eyes and dyed
my hair red as the sea Anastasia
Razor was raised by.

CHARLIE PETCH

## #48 COPPER RED

In case I die
a torn piece of hair-colour box
waits in my wallet with instructions
to get my roots done

the myth of Pinocchio
is that when he became a real boy
he was able to find happiness
but no one was interested
in his part two

behind that flesh and blood contentment
is the anvil of façade and fun
donkey boys bleating
a joy so enveloping
it could metamorphize

my nose never grew
when I started to dye my hair red
nor does a penis sprout from me
when I want to be a man

I was once strawberry blonde
but now I've muted into a
whispery whiney brown

so I will dye until death
a *damn I look great*
red #48
and wear a strap on

as telling as the nose
on Pinocchio's face

my body is a temple I build
from the top down
so that when I'm bottoms up
I will have lived
like a careening
red flag flying Ass
at a forever party

MARGARET ATWOOD

## 'NOBODY EVER DID WANT ME'

Lucy Maud Montgomery's novel *Anne of Green Gables* is 100-years-old this April, and the Annery is in full swing. Already there's a "prequel", Budge Wilson's *Before Green Gables*, which chronicles the life of spunky, strange, but endearing Anne Shirley before she hit Prince Edward Island's Green Gables farmhouse in a splatter of exclamation marks, apple blossoms, freckles and embarrassing faux pas. And there's yet another mutton-sleeved, button-booted, Gibson-girl-hairdo'ed television show in the offing—*Anne of Green Gables: A New Beginning*—due in 2009, following the 1919 silent film, the 1934 talkie, the 1956 television version, the 1979 Japanese animé, the 1985 *Green Gables* series, the 1990-96 *Road to Avonlea* and the PBS Animated Series of 2000, not to mention the various parodies—*Anne of Green Gut, Fran of the Fundy* and its brethren—that have appeared over the years.

On top of all that, a fresh edition of the first Anne book is available from the New Canadian Library, complete with the original illustrations. These are unsettling, as everyone in them has a very small head—Marilla in particular is not only pinheaded but practically bald—leading us to wonder about the degree of inbreeding that was going on around Avonlea. There's a curiously shaped Anne—more like a sort of Mary Poppins puppet than a girl—who turns into a pretty Dresden china figurine by book's end. But Anne's original image defects have been corrected over and over in the course of the century. In the many subsequent pictorial renditions of her, Anne's head returns to normal size—sometimes it gets a little too big—and the hair becomes much more prominent.

Nor is this process at an end: from the Anne of Green Gables Licensing Authority that gives the nod to all collateral products, expect more Anne boxed sets, Anne notepaper and Anne pencils, Anne coffee mugs and Anne aprons, Anne candies and Anne straw hats, and Anne—well, what else? Anne lace-edged pantaloon underclothing? Anne cookbooks—oops, we already have those. Talking Anne dolls that say, "You mean, hateful boy! How dare you!" followed by the sharp crack of a slate being broken over a thick skull, or else, "I hate you—I hate you—I hate you! You are a rude, unfeeling woman!" I always liked those parts.

For those of you who did not read this book as a child—are there any? Yes, and they are most likely male—Anne is the story of an orphaned, red-headed, freckled, 11-year-old girl who's been sent to the Green Gables farm in Avonlea by mistake. Marilla and Matthew Cuthbert, the elderly brother and sister who own the place, wanted a boy orphan to help with the chores, but eager, imaginative, drama-queen Anne makes such an impression on shy old bachelor Matthew—shown in the original illustrations as a dubious cross between Santa Claus and a tramp—that he wants her to stay, and tart, stern Marilla comes around to his way of thinking.

Anne's subsequent adventures, awkward scrapes, aesthetic hyperventilations and temper tantrums are both touching and amusing, as she grows from ugly-duckling waif to talented and beautiful swan, having dyed her hair temporarily green in the meantime. Ultimately, she wins the admiration and affection not only of Marilla, but of just about everyone in Avonlea except the girl we love to hate, whose name is Josie Pye. Finally, there's a bittersweet ending, wherein the wonderful Matthew dies—killed by a heart attack brought on by the shock of a failing bank that wipes out all his savings, thus giving us An Anne For Our Times—and scholarship-winning Anne renounces her larger college ambitions, at least for a while. She stays at Green Gables to help Marilla, who's at risk of going blind and would have to sell the place otherwise. This is the part where you really cry a lot.

The book was an instant success when it first appeared—Anne "is the dearest and most loveable child in fiction since the immortal Alice", growled crusty, cynical Mark Twain—and it's been going strong ever since. Anne has inspired many imitations: her more genuine literary descendents surely include Pippi Longstocking, not to mention Sailor Moon—girls who kick over the traces, but not too much. Montgomery herself wrote a string of sequels—*Anne of Avonlea*, *Anne of the Island*, *Anne's House of Dreams* and more; but the grown-up Anne is not the same, and neither is Avonlea after the outbreak of the first world war. As a child reader, I felt about these later books much as I felt about Wendy growing up at the end of *Peter Pan*. I didn't want to know.

*Anne of Green Gables* was first published in 1908, a year before my mother was born, so when I first grinned and snivelled my way through it at the age of eight, it was a youthful 40. I revisited it through the eyes of my own child in the 1980s, when it was approaching 80. Then our family actually went to Prince Edward Island, and stayed in Charlottetown, and saw the sprightly, upbeat Anne of Green Gables musical that's been running there continuously since 1965. I enjoyed it a lot, but watching a show about an 11-year-old girl with some real 11-year-old girls casts a different light on things: some of that enjoyment was vicarious.

We didn't buy any Anne dolls or cookbooks, nor did we visit the "Green Gables" facsimile farmhouse, which—judging from online accounts of it— is as complete as Sherlock Holmes's digs on Baker Street, containing everything from the slate Anne broke over Gilbert Blythe's head to her wardrobe of puffed-sleeve dresses to the brooch she was accused, wrongly, of losing. There's even a pretend Matthew who gives you drives around the property, though he's not described as running to hide out in the barn at the approach of lady visitors, as the real Matthew would have done. Now I wish I'd taken in more of these sights while I had the chance, though somewhere along the way we did check out the early 20th-century one-room schoolhouse where the high double desks were just like the ones Anne would have known.

From the point of view of the Annery, we were unsatisfactory consumers, though the many Japanese tourists who'd come a very long way to see the musical were snapping up the dolls, straw hats, books and aprons with encouraging briskness. I worried about these tourists during the musical itself—wouldn't the egg-and-spoon race present an insuperable cultural barrier?—but I needn't have. Anne's popularity in Japan (and she's been extremely popular) used to be a mystery to me. Then I went to Japan, and was able to ask a Japanese audience to explain Anne's fascination for them. There were thirty-two answers, all duly recorded by a nice lady who wrote them down, typed them out, and sent them to me. Here are some of them.

*Anne of Green Gables* was first translated by a Japanese author who was very well known and well loved already. Anne was an orphan and there were a lot of orphans in Japan right after the second world war, so many readers identified with her. Anne has a passion for apple blossoms and cherry blossoms—the latter are especially dear to the hearts of the Japanese—so her brand of aesthetic sensibility was very sympathetic. Anne had red hair, which—before the past twenty years or so, when even middle-aged Japanese ladies may sometimes be spotted with blue, green, red or orange hair—was thought to be extremely exotic. Anne is not only an orphan, but a poor girl orphan—the lowest of the low on the traditional Japanese social ladder. Yet she wins over that most formidable of Japanese dragons, the bossy older matron. (In fact, she wins over two of them, since she adds overbearing, opinionated, but good-at-heart Mrs Rachel Lynde to her collection basket.)

Anne has no fear of hard work: she's forgetful because dreamy, but she's not a shirker. She displays a proper attitude when she puts others before herself, and even more praiseworthy is that these others are elders. She has an appreciation of poetry, and although she shows signs of materialism—her longing for puffed sleeves is legendary—in her deepest essence, she's spiritual. And, high on the list, Anne breaks the Japanese taboo that forbade outbursts of temper on the part of young people. She acts out spectacularly, stamping her feet and hurling insults back at those who insult her, and even resorting to physical violence, most notably in the slate-over-the-head episode. This must have afforded much vicarious pleasure to young Japanese readers; indeed, to all Anne's young readers of yesteryear, so much more repressed than the children of today. Had they thrown scenes like the ones Anne throws, they would have got what my mother referred to as What For, or, if things were particularly bad, Hail Columbia. (I myself did not get What For or Hail Columbia, but they were a feature of my mother's stories about her own upbringing in rural Nova Scotia, which—as far as the schoolhouse and the churchgoing and the attitudes towards children went—was remarkably similar to Anne's.)

"God's in his heaven, all's right with the world," Anne whispers in the very last lines of *Anne of Green Gables*. She's fond of Victorian poetry, so it's appropriate that she ends her story by quoting from a song sung by the optimistic heroine of Robert Browning's dramatic poem "Pippa Passes"; doubly appropriate because Anne Shirley herself acts a kind of Pippa throughout the book. Pippa is a poor Italian orphan girl who slaves away in a silk-spinning mill, yet manages to preserve a pure imagination and a love of nature despite her lowly status. Like Pippa, Anne is an unselfconscious innocent who, unbeknownst to herself, brings joy, imagination and the occasional epiphany to the citizenry of Avonlea, who are inclined to be practical but drear.

It's unlikely that Anne Shirley would have been allowed to read all of

"Pippa Passes." Pippa's fellow characters are far from wholesome, and their doings are so sordid and explicitly sexual as to have caused moral outrage when the poem was first published: one of them is a mistress, and another has plans to debauch Pippa and lure her into a life of white slavery. Browning's view is the more realistic: in actual life, an orphaned girl like Anne would have had few prospects. "What a starved, unloved life she had had—a life of drudgery and poverty and neglect," thinks Marilla; and it's this starved, unloved life that Budge Wilson has explored in her "prequel". Judging from what we know about the lives of orphans at that time, including the many "London street Arabs", as Marilla calls them, that were being sent to Canada by the Barnardo homes, a statistically accurate Anne would have continued to be poor and neglected. However, through luck and her own merits, Anne is rescued by the Cuthbert siblings, thus joining a long line of redeemed fictional Victorian orphans, from *Jane Eyre* to *Oliver Twist* to little Tom the chimney sweep in Charles Kingsley's *The Water Babies*. Fairy-tale endings, we call these; for, in mythology and folklore, orphans were not merely downtrodden outsiders: they might be heroes-in-training, like King Arthur, or under the special protection of the gods or fairies. (There is certainly something uncanny about Anne—a "witch," she's often called—and a few centuries earlier she might well have been burnt at the stake.)

Outside of fiction, however, orphans weren't only exploited, they were feared and despised as fruits of sin: children with no identifiable fathers, resentful and even criminal Bad Seeds who'd do things like setting fire to people's houses "on purpose", as Rachel Lynde informs Marilla. This is why Montgomery goes to such lengths to provide Anne with two educated, respectable parents who were married to each other. But a real-life Anne would have led a Dickensian life of grinding child labour and virtual bondage as an unpaid mother's help—Anne has performed this function earlier in her life, once in a bare-bones backwoods household that sports three sets of twins. In my sourer moments, I confess to having imagined yet another Anne sequel, to be called Anne Goes on the Town. This would be a grim, Zolaesque epic that would chronicle the poor girl's enticement by means of puffed sleeves, then her sexual downfall and her subsequent brutal treatment at the hands of harsh male clients. Then would follow the pilfering of her ill-got though hard-earned gains by an evil madam, her dull despair self-medicated by alcohol and opium-smoking, and her sufferings from the ravages of an incurable STD. The final chapter would contain some Traviata-like coughing, her early and ugly death, and her burial in an unmarked grave, with nothing to mark the passing of this waif with a heart of gold but a volley of coarse jokes from her former customers. However, the presiding genius of Anne is not the gritty grey Angel of Realism, but the rainbow-coloured, dove-winged Godlet of the Heart's Desire. As Oscar Wilde said about second marriages, Anne is the triumph of hope over experience: it tells us not the truth about life, but the truth about wish fulfilment. And the main truth about wish fulfilment is that most people vastly prefer it to the alternative.

This is one of the reasons *Anne of Green Gables* has had such an ongoing life, but this in itself would hardly be enough: if Anne were nothing but a soufflé of happy thoughts and outcomes, the Annery would have collapsed long ago. The thing that distinguishes Anne from so many "girls' books" of the first half of the 20th century is its dark underside: this is what gives Anne its frenetic, sometimes quasi-hallucinatory energy, and what makes its heroine's idealism and indignation so poignantly convincing.

The dark side comes from the hidden life of Anne's author, LM Montgomery. Some of Montgomery's journals have been published, and several biographies have appeared, as well as a haunting 1975 television docudrama called *The Road to Green Gables*. There's a new biography due in October from Mary Henley Rubio—*The Gift of Wings: The Life of Lucy Maud Montgomery*—and doubtless in it we will learn even more about that hidden life, though what we know already is disheartening enough. Montgomery was a semi-orphan: her mother died when she was under two, and her father packed her off to be brought up by her strict Presbyterian grandparents in Cavendish, Prince Edward Island. The description of the chilly bedroom where Marilla puts Anne on her first night at Green Gables—a bedroom "of a rigidity not to be described in words, but which sent a shiver to the very marrow of Anne's bones"—is doubtless a metaphor for this household. Anne's plaintive cry, "You don't want me!…Nobody ever did want me", is a child's outraged protest against the unfairness of the universe that seems to come straight from the heart. Montgomery was an orphan sent to live with two old people, but, unlike Anne, she never did win them over. Marilla and Matthew are what Montgomery wished for, not what she got.

Anne's experiences minding other people's babies are bad enough—Marilla, "shrewd enough to read between the lines", pities her—but Montgomery's own experiences were, if anything, worse. The father she'd idealised from a distance moved out west and remarried, and Montgomery was sent for; but the joyful family reunion she must have anticipated didn't happen. Instead, she found herself kept out of school so she could tend the baby of her uncongenial new stepmother. Her father was seldom there.

Anne's precocious reading tastes and romantic imagination are similar to what we know of Montgomery's, but Montgomery did not star in a post-girlhood series of sequels in which she marries Gilbert Blythe. Instead, Montgomery went through two serious relationships: an engagement to a man she did not love, and a non-engagement to a man whom she loved passionately but couldn't bring herself to marry because he was an uneducated farmer. The farmer died, after which she renounced her romantic dreams and stayed home to look after her unpleasant grandmother. When she finally did marry, four months after the grandmother's death, she had premonitions of disaster—it's not a good omen to sit at your wedding breakfast feeling that it's your own funeral. Indeed, things did not work very well. Her husband, Ewen MacDonald, was a minister, and Montgomery had to perform the many tedious duties of a minister's wife, for which she was by no means as well suited as the beloved Mrs. Allan of Avonlea. But then Ewen began to suffer bouts of something then called "religious melancholia", but which today might be classified as clinical depression or even bipolar disorder, and Montgomery had to devote more and more time to his care. Later in her life, she herself suffered from nervous collapses, and no wonder. "Nobody ever did want me" was a burden imposed on her by her own childhood, and it proved a hard one to overcome. The many fictional worlds she created through her writing were both an escape from and a way of coming to terms with a deep underlying sadness.

There's another way of reading *Anne of Green Gables*, and that's to assume that the true central character is not Anne, but Marilla Cuthbert. Anne herself doesn't really change throughout the book. She grows taller, her hair turns from "carrots" to "a handsome auburn," her clothes get much prettier, due to the spirit of clothes competition she awakens in Marilla, she talks less, though more thoughtfully, but that's about it. As she herself says, she's still the same girl inside. Similarly, Matthew remains Matthew, and Anne's best chum Diana is equally static. Only Marilla unfolds into something unimaginable to us at the beginning of the book. Her growing love for Anne, and her growing ability to express that love—not Anne's duckling-to-swan act—is the real magic transformation. Anne is the catalyst who allows the crisp, rigid Marilla to finally express her long-buried softer human emotions. At the beginning of the book, it's Anne who does all the crying; by the end of it, much of this task has been transferred to Marilla. As Mrs. Rachel Lynde says, "Marilla Cuthbert has got mellow. That's what."

"I was wishing you could have stayed a little girl, even with all your queer ways," says Marilla in one of her weepy passages towards the end of the book. Marilla has finally allowed herself to make a wish, and now it's been granted: over the past hundred years, Anne has stayed the same. Good luck to her for the second hundred.

DIANE TUCKER

## TINY DRESSES

I'm sorry, Mum, for the dresses, all the tiny
dresses people gave you when I was a baby.
My infant skin, my redheaded skin,
hated their slippery nylon frills.
It itched, allergicked and rejected them.

Not the last time your odd daughter thwarted you.

Too many questions; I never shut up.
So many questions that they backed up
inside my mouth and came out stuttering, w-w-w-why?
Why d-d-d-darkness? Why d-d-d-death?

Too many feelings! How I howled when,
in *Mutual of Omaha's Wild Kingdom*, the lions
killed the zebra, bloodied its perfect stripes.
You weren't angry but you fussed and clucked.
Who was this, who cried over a TV show?
What were all those uncorkable *feelings*?

Too much cheek, sass, attitude.
At barely seven I learned to stick out my hip,
giggle and wink. How to flirt. I was no fool.
I saw the calendar ladies on the garage wall,
not covered enough with pickle jars of nails.
Dad would pass me long wood shavings, curls
as gold as Eva Gabor's hair, her tan breasts.

Too much putting two and two together:
this is what beautiful ladies are like;

this is what men like ladies to be like.
*Photoplay* and *Modern Screen* on the coffee table;
Women's Lib and Watergate on TV.
All those whirled together under my redheaded skin.

No wonder I itched and allergicked and rejected
the tiny dresses. My new body felt their synthetic
rasp, knew them costumes and threadbare.

## DOUBLE RECESSIVE

Excerpts from **Double Recessive**, a comedy, first performed as *Project Gingervitis* in 2014 at the Montreal Fringe Festival.

### Fashion Week

*In the near future...*

FASHION HOST:    It's award show season and time to see what's hot and what's not this year. There is Madonna looking sexy in a Chanel dress! And what does she have there? Of course, it's her recently adopted ginger son, Finnegan. So good of her to do that. Ginger kids are a very hot accessory right now. Paris Hilton just picked up a ginger son last month from Northern Ireland. Angelina got herself a little girl from Scotland, and not to be outdone, Kanye and Kim picked up a pair of twin boys from the Dublin demilitarized zone. Southern Asian kids are so 2007. African babies? What is this, 1993? Ginger kids are great because they provide that colourful pop that can complement almost any outfit. HOT!

These kids work best in the winter months, and especially with darker colours. Like an exotic Bengal tiger, a ginger kid will make you the talk of the town and a fashion force to be reckoned with. So, don't miss out! Get yourself a little ginger before it's too late and you have to put them away for the summer.

## Sunfox News 2: Interview with Simon, Subject Red 1

*Years after the genocide is complete it is revealed the government has been harbouring a single ginger individual in a secret laboratory.*

COOPER CHASE: We here at Sunfox news have the first exclusive interview with Subject Red 1. Do not be alarmed. You may find his appearance frightening. Tonight's program is not intended for young audiences and contains images some viewers may find disturbing. Ladies and gentlemen, Subject Red 1…

SIMON: Hello.

COOPER CHASE: Let's get right to it. You openly identify as a "ginger"?

SIMON: No, I don't really like that term, but everyone calls me that so I guess…

COOPER CHASE: So as a ginger, how responsible do you feel for the crimes of other gingers, such as Judas, Napoleon or Scott Thompson?

SIMON: I don't think I should feel responsible…

COOPER CHASE: Tell us about your skin condition. Are you able to go outside? Is the sun your enemy? It's been said that gingers, like vampires, only come out at night. That they will burn up if exposed to the sun.

SIMON: That's not true!

COOPER CHASE: But, a lot of people have said that gingers have no soul. Is *that* true?

SIMON:                     No. I mean…I don't think so…I don't know what
                           it feels like to not have a soul…

COOPER CHASE:              You're not sure if you have a soul? Do you believe
                           in god?

SIMON:                     I don't know what I believe.

COOPER CHASE:              Are all gingers ungodly? Are your people
                           inherently ungodly?

SIMON:                     No. I mean, I don't know.

COOPER CHASE:              I want to ask the question that I think is on
                           everyone's mind. Are you an agent of the devil?

SIMON (stands up):         No! I am not a devil! If you'll let me explain…

COOPER CHASE:              But, are you an *agent* of the devil?

SIMON:                     That's ridiculous! Can you let me talk for just one
                           second?

COOPER CHASE:              My god! Look at the fire in his eyes! He's like a wild
                           beast! *Clearly*, we're dealing with a creature that
                           is far more dangerous and unpredictable than we
                           could *ever* imagine.

                           Coming up next we'll be joined by our Sunfox
                           News threat assessment panel of experts for a more
                           in depth analysis of this *serious* and *disturbing*
                           threat. Stay tuned…

WINONA LINN

## RED FOX

This coat was a gift
that matches my hair
and begs an explanation:
*Winona, why?*

This coat is controversial.
I don't understand.
Pigs can solve puzzles
and octopi mourn their dead but we eat bacon and *tako*,
I don't.
I'm a fur-wearing vegetarian.
It's not hypocritical.

This coat is vintage.
The collar was killed in nineteen seventy-five
the sleeves in seventy-seven
both in August
when *Vulpes vulpes* was at her reddest
and slow with a belly of voles.

I am at my reddest, too
in August when the coat sleeps in cedar chips
and my skin matches my hair no matter how I hide from the sun.
I am an endangered species,
more vulnerable than the fox whose skin I wear·each winter.

Sunlight threatens me.
I pray for rain.

It will ruin my coat.

## SEEING RED

Kate Flynn had never been the violent type. But at this moment, sitting in a dim Italian restaurant with a fake smile pasted on her face, as she half-listened to a man drone on about his paleo diet, she was contemplating the perfect way to murder her best friend. A slow, agonizing death. She is, after all, the reason why this annoying man was sitting across from her.

"What's one evening?" Celia said over coffee the week before. "Carl might be the one."

Kate had ignored "*the one*" comment, but recognized the tiny spark of hope that flickered in her. "What do you know about him?"

"He likes redheads."

Right. Because that was enough? "And?"

Celia's hesitation should have been a red flag. "I don't know a lot about him, honestly. He's at CrossFit early mornings, so he must have a job to go to." She'd grinned. "And he's *really* hot. If I wasn't married..." Her words trailed off.

Kate tried not to smile, remembering the conversation. She focused on the man across from her. Celia was right, he was stunning—a chiseled jaw, thick, black hair, and killer blue eyes that made Kate's ovaries take notice.

"...should never eat carbs," he was saying, his reasoning lost among the din of the busy restaurant and Kate's meandering thoughts. "If you care about your body, I mean." He gave her a once-over and Kate, who worked hard for her yoga-fit body, suddenly felt uncomfortable, exposed.

She clenched her jaw as she looked down at her menu and took a few deep breaths. At least she didn't have to bother with conversation; he seemed happy to continue his monologue.

The waitress returned with their drinks—pinot grigio for her and a pretentious-sounding scotch for him. She asked if they were ready to order.

Kate closed her menu. "I'll have the fettuccine alfredo, please."

She heard a gurgle from the other side of the table that she suspected was Carl swallowing his tongue. "Don't forget the garlic bread," she added, smothering a smirk.

"Are you sure that's what you want? Pasta *and* bread coated in *dairy*?" Carl asked. The word *dairy* may as well have been *excrement*, the way he said it.

Kate pinned him with her eyes. "One hundred percent sure," she said, not caring, no, *hoping* he was offended.

Instead, he gave her a condescending smile. "Don't worry, honey, I can teach you how to better fuel your body."

Forcing herself to unclench her fists, Kate removed the napkin from her lap and politely excused herself while Carl ordered his steak.

Barely inside the bathroom, Kate pulled out her phone and banged out an angry text: *Total douche. Bailing.*

Her phone rang. Kate dispensed with a greeting. "You are going to die a very slow death," she declared

"Tell me," Celia said. After Kate finished, Celia sighed. "Ugh. I wouldn't blame you if you bailed. And stopped being my friend. I'm so sorry."

Kate laughed. "It helps that you're contrite."

"He seemed so nice at the gym."

*Don't they all*, Kate thought. "Well, I'd better get back out there before he thinks I snuck out the window. I'll just tell him I was doing squats or something."

She returned to the table, thinking about an exit strategy. Ordering the most paleo-offensive meal hadn't worked to turn this guy off; she needed to up her game.

"I missed you," he said as she replaced the napkin in her lap. She looked up just as his hand came toward her. Her entire body stiffened as he coiled one of her curls around a finger. "I love your hair, by the way."

*I swear to God*, Kate thought, *if you ask me if the carpet matches the drapes, I will gouge your eyes out with my pasta spoon.*

Her eyes darted around, looking for some way to get out of this. There was a man sitting alone at the bar. He wore a white dress shirt and dark pants, his workaday outfit unremarkable. What was remarkable was the colour of his hair, which was identical to her own.

Her gaze must have lingered because Carl swiveled his head to follow it. "Is that your brother?"

Kate's attention was drawn back. "Because all redheads are related?"

He shrugged.

Maybe for the first time since this Neanderthal had opened his mouth, Kate smiled and relaxed a little. "Actually, funny thing: that *is* my brother. Give me a second to say hi."

Her date reached for his glass of scotch, pretentiously swirling it as she walked past him. A few minutes later, Kate returned to the table. "You don't mind if my brother, Dennis, joins us for a bit, do you?"

Carl stood, and the men shook hands. "Not at all. You look like you work out. Nice."

"Er… thanks?" Dennis glanced at Kate awkwardly.

Kate smirked at him as if to say: *See? Told you.*

Carl grabbed a chair from the empty table beside them, waving the new arrival toward it.

Would *anything* clue this guy in? What woman would invite her brother to sit with her and a guy on a date?

In a last-ditch effort, Kate turned toward Dennis and said, "I'm so glad we ran into you tonight. I've been so lonely since I last saw you at Thanksgiving."

Before Dennis could respond, she wrapped a palm around the back of his neck, and pulled him in for a kiss. It started as a sisterly kiss. Then it wasn't.

Carl gurgled, causing Kate to smile against Dennis's lips.

Dennis's hand rose to Kate's cheek as they kissed. Like lovers.

"What the—?" Carl exclaimed in disgust.

Kate slowly pulled away and turned toward him. "What's wrong?" she asked in the most innocent of voices.

"*What's wrong?*" he sputtered. Not waiting for an answer, he stood, uttered some unintelligible noises, and then made a brisk exit.

Kate exhaled in relief, not even caring that she'd be stuck with the bill. "Finally. God that guy… Thank you."

Dennis smiled. "Sure thing."

"No point wasting a meal," she said. "Do you enjoy steak?"

"Sure do," Dennis returned the extra chair to its rightful place before taking the seat across from her. "Almost as much as I enjoy incest."

Kate barked out a laugh, but then added, "I'm sorry, but I've already forgotten your last name." With a wink, she added, "Brother."

"Sheffield."

"Good to meet you, Dennis Sheffield."

"Likewise," he said with a grin.

Kate reached for her wine glass and raised it high. "Here's to family."

JENNIFER ZILM

## WEST COAST LETTER TO MY GINGER TWIN
*for Shannon*


Oh well, another year,
another translation
of the old German
misery goat's castle elegies
and I remember suddenly
you saying you were done
with male lyric poets—a fist
in your crispy ginger curls,
mouth red wine and wine lipstick—
a tiny booted foot stamping
on my hardwood floor for emphasis.
So now in the margins
I am proclaiming (in pink sharpie)
the International Year of the Elegy.
I am listing every uppercase noun
in a stolen Chapters' rose-window
bound notebook. What time is it
where you are right now? And don't say
 a quarter past a freckle. After a morning
of archival description and a year of culling
my sister's set of German flashcards,
I am riding the #7 gratefully
mourning the missing rain
(it's Vancouver, it's November!),
gleefully loving the death
of the bus detour, how easily
again Powell becomes Cordova,
the turn up Main (as is fitting:
as the electric wires have
determined it) and I'm ready

to be added to the pile
of grave girls (translation:
*I'm so happy I could die*).
Oh my ginger twin, Mädchen,
please send a letter with many ellipses
bracketing your signature phrase this, that
and the other thing. Compose
my elegy as piece of item-level,
non-hierarchical description.
If at all possible, please display
my fonds beneath a bell jar
in field of a crop
of your choosing.

# GINGER SPICE

# CALICO

**Red**
Picture of me propped up, weeks old,
red wisps an angel's pass,
my dad's disappointment a shadow yet to fall
over the next photo as I fade to blonde,
broken legacy, me;
what I would give later to have stayed red,
to be Anne in place of Anita,
unfolding poetic in Diana's arms,
a rose in place of a lily,
a dagger in place of a bow.

**Blonde**
We don't have the most fun,
just suffer the most punchlines.
None of us are what you think
we don't care what you think but we have to.
I'm a thought of big tits and bouncing hair—
double dare you to hear a whole sentence
coming from my blah, blah, blah.

**Brunette**
Baby, this is it, suits me perfect.
We're in business now, on fire.
How'd I never think of this before?
This is freedom. Sexy freedom. Skin
like moonlight, hair mahogany, I'm like
furniture. I look like fucking furniture.
Baby, wash me out.

## White

An isolated incident, freak of poor design,
silver thread at 18, a web by 35;
my mother's hair, her nature, too.
I grow calico as I get older,
strawberry and ice, grey and yellow,
sun-bleach and streaks of limelight. "Please don't ask me
to dye this, Honey," my stylist pleads, ankles wobbling
atop five-inch suede stilettos. Don't you know
people pay good money to look like you these days?

## Orange

I give birth to a ginger baby,
boy and a conduit,
colour that lasts,
hand-me-down genes that stay handed,
more my family than me
a tinderbox of red will and wit.
At seven, he says "It's really more orange.
Why's everyone call it red?"
Your guess is as good as mine, kid.
Maybe it's a metaphor.

CAROLYN CLINK

## SUPPER WITH THE SPHINX

I say: *Girl,*
*what are you waiting for?*
She always answers:
a man.

The Sphinx orders octopus
or sometimes escargot
but never an animal
with four, two, or three legs.

*You're a Leo,*
*a red-maned lion-woman,*
*you don't need a man*
*to solve your problems.*

At a relationship crossroad,
she's dumped another carcass
in her all-you-can-eat-buffet
love life.

*And what if you find*
*this one man?* Then, she says,
she can truly die happy.
Now, for dessert.

She questions the server.
His answers do not satisfy,
but she likes this restaurant.
She lets him live.

## THISTLE

The ride back from the restaurant was quiet until Lista drove over the wooden planks of the Old Mill Bridge. She slowed the truck and turned to the right into a hidden lane that slipped out of sight between a grove of poplars.

"What are we doing here?" asked Herb Thistle.

"I don't know about you, but I'm going for a swim," she said, shifting into reverse, turning off the key and climbing out of the truck.

"I don't have a bathing suit. And anyway, you have to wait an hour after eating."

She gave him a withering look through the open window. "That's just something mothers say. It's not true."

He watched her descend the dirt embankment on an angle, sidestepping until she reached the sandy shore of the stream below. She was very light on her feet, graceful even. She looked back and then moved to where he could only see her upper body. By her movements, he could tell she had removed her heavy boots, then her cargo pants. Next came her shirt and she had nothing beneath. She moved toward the water, wading in until she found her footing then smoothly glided forward.

He held his breath. The contrasts—her red hair, white shoulders against the clear water. Her body opening and closing like a jellyfish as she swam into the dappled pool beneath the overhanging huckleberry bushes. He saw glistening flashes of her as she porpoised in the current.

A quarter of an hour later when she emerged sleek from the water, he averted his eyes and got out of the truck, slamming the door. He stalked back up through the grove and threw himself down with his back against a poplar and hugged his knees. He should have joined her—dropped his pants and let her see his gimpy leg. So what! All his life he had avoided the limelight and used his gimpy leg as his crutch. Can't play baseball, see, I have this injury. Swim? Can't do that either. The lame leg was smaller than the other, noticeably so, which is why he hid it away like a family secret. In his heart of hearts, he was Tarzan, roaring and swinging tree to tree in search of adventure. Two good legs and afraid of nothing. That had to be sublimated in order to survive. Not thrive, but survive. He rolled himself upright and returned to the truck.

Lista sat behind the wheel, braiding her hair. "Don't you love this place? The sound the bridge makes as cars thump across those old planks. The sun slanting through the trees like that." Her hair held prisms of light and she looked serene as she faced him, hand on the key in the ignition. "Why didn't you come in?"

Herb looked out the side window and didn't reply. He wouldn't tell her how good she looked—a constellation of new freckles across her face. Redheads don't do well under close scrutiny, she had warned him.

"You don't skinny dip?"

"No, and just leave it at that."

She backed the truck between the trees and turned it around. "You're a strange dude."

"So I've been told."

Her shirt stuck to her damp skin and she plucked it away from her breasts. "That was a good swim. I feel better. You could have come in, you know. I wouldn't have looked. Well, I probably would have."

## FOXGLOVE

The darkest days have yet to find me
Reaching my 80th year without absolution
Lucent still hunts me
Relentless in his pursuit
His hunger for revenge, unstoppable
My past heroic feats a charade
Symbiosis of the truth, my fate

Days gone by in a spiral of memories
I was once regaled by the media
Super hero, a champion to young girls
My metropolis slept sound
Nocturnal, I purged the streets
Trapping vermin in 4 by 10 cages
Gold leaf chalice, brim-filled liquid victory

The calling of your name is foreboding
Pulling me fathoms below the silt
A challenge I could not win
Without clear retribution
In the eyes of the dwellers
Failure a sinner's badge sewn deep
Repose masking my shame

My wet ginger hair matted
Skin flushed with hard coded guilt
Wondering how the coroner's slab will feel
Night's lost to obsessing my demise
Will you quietly stalk me

Or stand with me face to face
As you stab me in the back

I was for many years sybarite
Exquisite deliciousness a heroic afterglow
Until you drove me underground
Years of reclusive existence
A sandwich shop, escape into the outside
Dark stairwells & alleyways a cover
Helping me blend into walls

Your hunt for me, relentless, driven
The hunger of a werewolf about to feast
You tried to flush me out
Covering my scent, I evaded
Dead end trails, stirring your fury
Sacrificing your own, for my demise
Waking hours spent in pursuit

Decades passing, yet time stands still
Your stature even grander
My aged body, cannot manoeuvre with grace
To survive, my wits must whip you
In recognia, a fighter's stance, reflex
Then you smell my fired blood
Your desire to end me, blinds you

No gracious end in our final battle
Will defenestrated, cast to Hades & purgatory
You will cry gravitas & I words of revenge
Your power removed with each blow I lay
Cherrywood cane the ultimate weapon
Blade embedded in shaft, plunged deep
Your final breath, my escape from eternal hell

## ONCE A REDHEAD

I'd just come from a talking to in Brian's office and had promised him no fuck-ups, no scenes, no flouncing off shift in a huff. "Halloween is going to be a gong show," he'd said. "And I need my two best bartenders up there. You're gonna be okay working together, yeah?"

Obviously, Jamie had blabbed about us. How much did Brian know, besides the fact that I was twenty-six to Jamie's nineteen? Had Jamie told him we'd done it in the bushes at Ontario Place? In my car. The chair in one of the busboy's dad's home office where we'd sneaked off to screw while everyone else lay sprawled on the rec room floor listening to Guns N' Roses. I'd been off my face but vaguely recall said dad catching us *in flagrante*. Pretty juvenile shit. I bet Signe didn't know.

Brian watched me from across the bar as I grabbed a coffee and slid into the booth across from the lovebirds. To discuss Halloween costumes. To prove how adult I was. "I have this great idea."

They didn't even look my way. Jamie was making a performance out of her hair. Stroking it. Winding her mahogany corkscrew curls around his fingers, rubbing the tips over his lips like a paintbrush. You'd think she was the first redhead to walk the earth. Or the last.

"My mother has auburn hair." I lit two cigarettes and passed Jamie one to break the spell Signe was casting. A fug of smoke drifted up from the booth. "Had. It fades as you get older."

He teased a curl and her hair jiggled, a mass of tiny red springs. More burnt umber than red, really.

"How about Pebbles and Bamm Bamm?" I said.

"You," he licked her face, nibbled at her ear, "would make such a cute Pebbles." She turned and nosed him like a seal.

"*Staff* costumes. We're the main attraction, Jamie." *Charleston's* '80s style platform bar sat centre stage, stools flanked all four sides. Nowhere to hide. "We should be the ones who match."

"Jude's right," Signe said. "Everyone will get a kick out of seeing you guys coordinated."

"You could come as Raggedy Ann." I blew smoke her way. "Or Jessica Rabbit." Signe blinked her watery eyes. "Wendy from Wendy's." Jamie frowned at me across the table.

"We can run-up the costumes ourselves." By *we* I meant *me*. But I said *we*, rolling the word around in my mouth like a spoonful of oil. "I have a sewing machine. I used to make all my own clothes." Once I'd made a dress in home ec.

We arranged to meet in the parking lot at Fabricland. In the light of day, Signe's skin appeared translucent, flawless beneath the makeup she wasn't wearing. Like she'd burn in strong moonlight.

Jamie and I shared a cigarette after which I sashayed around the store stroking bolts of fabrics and tossing words over my shoulder I had only a hazy notion of: bias, selvedge, inlay, ease. They trailed behind, arms so tight around each other it was a wonder they could walk. His hand caressing her hip back ass shoulders neck. Her wondrous fucking hair.

I chose plain black for Pebble's shorts and white fleece for the top. An orange cotton remnant for Bamm Bamm's loincloth on which Signe offered to paint leopard spots. We piled into my car, Signe calling out directions from the back seat how to get to Jamie's parents' house. She was such a nice kid. I couldn't picture her getting mad about anything. Maybe I was just useless at reading her. Would touching him rouse her possessiveness? Stir some latent fiery temper? Using jeans and a t-shirt from his clean laundry pile, I roughed out a paper template.

When I returned from the drugstore on Saturday, my mother followed me into the bathroom. "I had beautiful auburn hair when I was your age."

"So you keep saying." I closed the door in her face.

"Read the instructions carefully," she called out.

Afterwards she poured olive oil on a cotton ball and helped me rub the stains from my neck and hairline. We didn't talk about how sallow my skin looked. The way the cartoon orange sucked up the light in the room, casting baleful shadows that distorted the planes of my face; changed my whole personality.

"Redheads are more sensitive to pain," she said.

As my hair was too short to scrape into a Pebbles' do, I fastened one of Bear's rawhide bones in a half-up ponytail on the crown of my head. Dotted freckles across my cheeks, and having run out of time for Pebble's shorts, made do with winding the dark fabric diaper-like across my hips and between my legs. I waddled to my car, Bamm Bamm's costume in the Shopper's Drug Mart plastic bag. As I turned to reverse down the driveway, the too tight sleeves on Pebble's top cut off the circulation in my arms.

When he saw my get-up, Jamie said, "You don't watch much TV, do you?" Then, "What the fuck, Jude?" His chest and shoulders had filled out since I'd last run my fingers over them. Front and back, Bamm Bamm's outfit barely skimmed the hem of his underwear. Brian whistled as he walked by with the bar float. I hitched my sagging diaper and a couple of stitches popped under my arms. How had I gotten everything so wrong? Our shift began in ten minutes.

We were three deep at the bar, the dance floor heaving when Signe parted the crowd in a skin-tight, ankle-grazing, green sequined dress that belied her age. She must have spent hours blow-drying her hair into Rita Hayworth waves. But there was barely time to ooh and aah. Costume restrictions aside, we were efficiency in motion, scooping glasses dripping wet from the glass-washer, lining them up and pouring: Caesars, fuzzy navels, B52s, blowjobs, sex-on-the-beach, brain hemorrhages. Bamm Bamm bent to grab a beer and the girls hollered. A stitch popped every time I reached to pull a pint. Our tip jar overflowed.

The dj lined up Rick James. Bamm Bamm shouted across the bar. "It's your song, Jude."

*Super freak, super freak*, everyone chorused to my pumping fist. I, the girl no one took home, did a twirl and wagged a finger to my adlib, "Uh uh, not to your mother." The bar roared and whistled and Brian had to run over with the First Aid kit and fish out the safety pins so I could wiggle my bum some more. I owned that song. Meanwhile, Signe shimmered like some exotic underwater creature, sipping on a grasshopper. A seashell winked from her cascade of red waves. I brushed sweat from my forehead and the back of my hand came away orange.

There's a picture of the staff taken long after last call. I'm wearing some-one else's sweats, someone else's hat on my head, tipped like I'm in Michael

Jackson's Billie Jean video. You can see trickles of red on my neck. Signe and Bamm Bamm are absent, probably Bamm Bamming in his narrow smelly bed.

I quit my job long before the three months it took the temporary red to fade. A humiliating fling with a married man convinced me a break in Europe might be a good idea. More than a year passed before I walked into *Charleston's* again. Jamie looked different, lesser somehow. And it wasn't just his prematurely thinning hair and receding hairline, the shot and beer chaser he was nursing, or how quickly he'd become some sad fixture on the other side of the bar. One drink led to old-time's sake and we ended up in bed before the night was out. But he was no longer my young conquest. And in his now expert hands and tongue, in the way he moved his body, and moved mine, the way he held his broken heart just out of my reach, I knew she was still there, her red hair splayed on the pillow between us.

CARLA HARTSFIELD

## YOU AND MY HAIR

I promised I wouldn't cut my hair
before Valentine's. Even as the words floated
from my mouth, I wanted to forget this vow,
kiss you instead, let the uncut
tendrils fall about your face.
*Who said anything about cutting hair?*

We made love this morning.
As I burrow beneath the sheets,
Wiarton Willy scuttles from his home.
It's Groundhog Day and the crowd cheers
at the fiction of an early spring.
I'm spurred on to write a love poem,
to shear these copper locks.

Why are all my lovers obsessed
with the electric threads of hair
left behind on pillows?
When the men find these unintentional gifts,
they think they own me.

As I dream the mass of red
falling onto my stylist's floor,
soon swept away, I imagine
a well-timed delivery truck,
and twelve rose-heads shorn.

# HAIRBALL

On the thirteenth of November, day of the unluck, month of the dead, Kat went into the Toronto General Hospital for an operation. It was for an ovarian cyst, a large one.

Many women had them, the doctor told Kat. Nobody knew why. There wasn't any way of finding out whether the thing was malignant, whether it contained, already, the spores of her death. Not before they went in. He spoke of "going in" the way she'd heard old veterans in TV documentaries speak of assaults on enemy territory. There was the same tensing of the jaw, the same fierce gritting of the teeth, the same grim enjoyment. Except that what he would be going into was her body. Counting down, waiting for the anesthetic, Kat, too, gritted her teeth fiercely. She was terrified, but she was also curious. Curiosity has got her through a lot.

She'd made the doctor promise to save the thing for her, whatever it was, so she could have a look. She was intensely interested in her own body, in anything it might choose to do or produce; although when flaky Dania, who did layout at the magazine, told her this growth was a message to her from her body, and she ought to sleep with an amethyst under the pillow to calm her vibrations, Kat told her to stuff it.

The cyst turned out to be a benign tumor. Kat liked that use of "benign," as if the thing had a soul and wished her well. It was big as a grapefruit, the doctor said. "Big as a coconut," said Kat. Other people had grapefruits. "Coconut" was better. It conveyed the hardness of it, and the hairiness, too.

The hair in it was red-long strands of it wound round and round inside, like a ball of wet wool gone berserk or like the guck you pull out of a clogged bathroom-sink drain. There were little bones in it, too, or fragments of bone-bird bones, the bones of a sparrow crushed by a car. There was a scattering of nails, toe or finger. There were five perfectly formed teeth.

"Is this abnormal?" Kat asked the doctor, who smiled. Now that he had gone in and come out again, unscathed, he was less clenched.

"Abnormal? No," he said carefully, as if breaking the news to a mother about a freakish accident to her newborn. "Let's just say it's fairly common." Kat was a little disappointed. She would have preferred uniqueness.

She asked for a bottle of formaldehyde, and put the cut open tumor into it. It was hers, it was benign, it did not deserve to be thrown away. She took it back to her apartment and stuck it on the mantelpiece. She named it Hairball. It isn't that different from having a stuffed bear's head or a preserved ex-pet or anything else with fur and teeth looming over your fireplace; or she pretends it isn't. Anyway, it certainly makes an impression.

Ger doesn't like it. Despite his supposed yen for the new and outré, he is a squeamish man. The first time he comes around (sneaks around, creeps around) after the operation, he tells Kat to throw Hairball out. He calls it "disgusting." Kat refuses point-blank, and says she'd rather have Hairball in a bottle on her mantelpiece than the soppy dead flowers he's brought her, which will anyway rot a lot sooner than Hairball will. As a mantelpiece ornament, Hairball is far superior. Ger says Kat has a tendency to push things to extremes, to go over the edge, merely from a juvenile desire to shock, which is hardly a substitute for wit. One of these days, he says, she will go way too far. Too far for him is what he means.

"That's why you hired me, isn't it?" she says. "Because I go way too far." But he's in one of his analyzing moods. He can see these tendencies of hers reflected in her work on the magazine, he says. All that leather and those grotesque and tortured looking poses are heading down a track he and others are not at all sure they should continue to follow. Does she see what he means, does she take his point? It's a point that's been made before. She shakes her head slightly, says nothing. She knows how that translates: there have been complaints from the advertisers. Too bizarre, too kinky. Tough.

"Want to see my scar?" she says. "Don't make me laugh, though. You'll crack it open." Stuff like that makes him dizzy: anything with a hint of blood, anything gynecological. He almost threw up in the delivery room, when his wife had a baby two years ago. He'd told her that with pride. Kat thinks about sticking a cigarette into the side of her mouth, as in a black-and-white movie of the forties. She thinks about blowing the smoke into his face.

Her insolence used to excite him during their arguments.

Then there would be a grab of her upper arms, a smoldering, violent kiss.

He kisses her as if he thinks someone else is watching him and judging the image they make together. Kissing the latest thing, hard and shiny, purple-mouthed, crop-headed; kissing a girl, a woman, a girl in a little crotch-hugger skirt and skintight leggings. He likes mirrors.

But he isn't excited now. And she can't decoy him into bed; she isn't ready for that yet, she isn't healed. He has a drink, which he doesn't finish, holds her hand as an afterthought, gives her a couple of avuncular pats on the off-white out-sized alpaca shoulder, leaves too quickly.

"Goodbye, Gerald," she says. She pronounces the name with mockery. It's a negation of him, an abolishment of him, like ripping a medal off his chest. It's a warning.

He'd been Gerald when they first met. It was she who transformed him, first to Gerry, then to Ger. (Rhymed with "flair," rhymed with "dare.") She made him get rid of those sucky pursed-mouth ties, told him what shoes to wear, got him to buy a loose-cut Italian suit, redid his hair. A lot of his current tastes—in food, in drink, in recreational drugs, in women's entertainment underwear—were once hers. In his new phase, with his new, hard, stripped-down name ending on the sharpened note of "r," he is her creation.

As she is her own. During her childhood, she was a romanticized Katherine, dressed by her misty-eyed, fussy mother in dresses that looked like ruffled pillowcases. By high school, she'd shed the frills and emerged as a bouncy, round-faced Kathy, with gleaming freshly washed hair and enviable teeth, eager to please and no more interesting than a health-food ad. At university she was Kath, blunt and no-bullshit in her Take-Back-the-Night jeans and checked shirt and her bricklayer-style striped denim peaked hat. When she ran away to England, she sliced herself down to Kat. It was economical, street-feline, and pointed as a nail. It was also unusual. In England you had to do something to get their attention, especially if you weren't English. Safe in this incarnation, she Ramboed through the eighties.

It was the name, she still thinks, that got her the interview, and then the job. The job was with an avant-garde magazine, the kind that was printed on matte stock in black and white, with overexposed closeups of women with hair blowing over their eyes, one nostril prominent: *The Razor's Edge*, it was called. Haircuts as art, some real art, film reviews, a little stardust, wardrobes of ideas that were clothes and of clothes that were ideas—the metaphysical shoulder pad. She learned her trade well, hands-on. She learned what worked.

She made her way up the ladder, from layout to design, then to the supervision of whole spreads, and then whole issues. It wasn't easy, but it was worth it. She had become a creator; she created total looks. After a while, she could walk down the street in Soho or stand in the lobby at openings and witness her handiwork incarnate, strolling around in outfits she'd put together, spouting her warmed-over pronouncements. It was like being God, only God had never got around to off-the-rack lines.

By that time her face had lost its roundness, though the teeth, of course, remained: there was something to be said for North American dentistry. She'd shaved off most of the hair, worked on the drop-dead stare, perfected a certain turn of the neck that conveyed an aloof inner authority. What you had to make them believe was that you knew something they didn't know yet. What you also had to make them believe was that they, too, could know this thing, this thing that would give them eminence and power and sexual allure, would attract envy to them—but for a price. The price of the magazine. What they could never get through their heads was that it was done entirely with cameras. Frozen light, frozen time. Given the angle, she could make any woman look ugly. Any man, as well. She could make anyone look beautiful, or at least interesting. It was all photography, it was all iconography. It was all in the choosing eye. This was the thing that could never be bought, no matter how much of your pitiful monthly wage you blew on snakeskin.

Despite the status, *The Razor's Edge* was fairly low-paying. Kat herself could not afford many of the things she contextualized so well. The grittiness and expense of London began to get to her; she got tired of gorging on the canapés at literary launches in order to scrimp on groceries, tired of the fuggy smell of cigarettes ground into the red-and-maroon carpeting of pubs, tired of the pipes bursting every time it froze in winter, and of the Clarissas and Melissas and Penelopes at the magazine rabbiting on about how they had been literally, absolutely, totally freezing all night, and how it literally, absolutely, totally, usually never got that cold. It always got that cold. The pipes always burst. Nobody thought of putting in real pipes, ones that would not burst next time. Burst pipes were an English tradition, like so many others.

Like, for instance, English men. Charm the knickers off you with their mellow vowels and frivolous verbiage, and then, once they'd got them off, panic and run. Or else stay and whinge. The English called it "whinging" instead of whining. It was better, really. Like a creaking hinge. It was a traditional compliment to be whinged at by an Englishman. It was his way of saying he trusted you, he was conferring upon you the privilege of getting to know the real him. The inner, whinging him. That was how they thought of women, really: whinge receptacles. Kat could play it, but that didn't mean she liked it.

She had an advantage over the English women, though: she was of no class. She had no class. She was in a class of her own. She could roll around among the English men, all different kinds of them, secure in the knowledge that she was not being measured against the class yardsticks and accent detectors they carried around in their back pockets, was not subject to the petty snobberies and resentments which lent such richness to their inner lives. The flip side of this freedom was that she was beyond the pale. She was a colonial—how fresh, how vital, how anonymous, how finally of no consequence. Like a hole in the wall, she could be told all secrets and then abandoned with no guilt.

She was too smart, of course. The English men were very competitive; they liked to win. Several times it hurt. Twice she had abortions, because the men in question were not up for the alternative. She learned to say that she didn't want children anyway, that if she longed for a rug rat she would buy a gerbil. Her life began to seem long. Her adrenaline was running out. Soon she would be thirty, and all she could see ahead was more of the same.

This was how things were when Gerald turned up. "You're terrific," he said, and she was ready to hear it, even from him, even though "terrific" was a word that had probably gone out with fifties crewcuts. She was ready for his voice by that time, too: the flat, metallic, nasal tone of the Great Lakes, with its clear hard "r"s and its absence of theatricality. Dull normal. The speech of her people. It came to her suddenly that she was an exile.

Gerald was scouting, Gerald was recruiting. He'd heard about her, looked at her work, sought her out. One of the big companies back in Toronto was launching a new fashion-oriented magazine, he said: up-market, international in its coverage, of course, but with some Canadian fashion in it, too, and with lists of stores where the items portrayed could actually be bought. In that respect, they felt they'd have it all over the competition, those American magazines that assumed you could only get Gucci in New York or Los Angeles. Heck, times had changed, you could get it in Edmonton! You could get it in Winnipeg!

Kat had been away too long. There was Canadian fashion now? The English quip would be to say that "Canadian fashion" was an oxymoron. She refrained from making it, lit a cigarette with her cyanide-green Covent Garden-boutique leather-covered lighter (as featured in the May issue of *The Razor's Edge*), looked Gerald in the eye. "London is a lot to give up," she said levelly. She glanced around the see-me-here Mayfair restaurant where they were finishing lunch, a restaurant she'd chosen because she'd known he was paying. She'd never spend that kind of money on food otherwise. "Where would I eat?"

Gerald assured her that Toronto was now the restaurant capital of Canada. He himself would be happy to be her guide. There was a great Chinatown, there was world-class Italian. Then he paused, took a breath. "I've been meaning to ask you," he said. "About the name. Is that Kat as in Krazy?" He thought this was suggestive. She'd heard it before.

"No," she said. "It's Kat as in KitKat. That's a chocolate bar. Melts in your mouth." She gave him her stare, quirked her mouth, just a twitch.

Gerald became flustered, but he pushed on. They wanted her, they needed her, they loved her, he said in essence. Someone with her fresh, innovative approach and her experience would be worth a lot of money to them, relatively speaking. But there were rewards other than the money. She would be in on the initial concept, she would have a formative influence, she would have a free hand. He named a sum that made her gasp, inaudibly of course. By now she knew better than to betray desire.

So she made the journey back, did her three months of culture shock, tried the world-class Italian and the great Chinese, and seduced Gerald at the first opportunity, right in his junior vice-presidential office. It was the first time Gerald had been seduced in such a location, or perhaps ever. Even though it was after hours, the danger frenzied him. It was the idea of it. The daring. The image of Kat kneeling on the broadloom in a legendary bra that until now he'd seen only in the lingerie ads of the Sunday *New York Times*, unzipping him in full view of the silver-framed engagement portrait of his wife that complemented the impossible ballpoint-pen set on his desk. At that time he was so straight he felt compelled to take off his wedding ring and place it carefully in the ashtray first. The next day he brought her a box of David Wood Food Shop chocolate truffles. They were the best, he told her, anxious that she should recognize their quality. She found the gesture banal, but also sweet. The banality, the sweetness, the hunger to impress: that was Gerald.

Gerald was the kind of man she wouldn't have bothered with in London. He was not funny, he was not knowledgeable, he had little verbal charm. But he was eager, he was tractable, he was blank paper. Although he was eight years older than she was, he seemed much younger. She took pleasure in his furtive, boyish delight in his own wickedness. And he was so grateful. "I can hardly believe this is happening," he said, more frequently than was necessary and usually in bed.

His wife, whom Kat encountered (and still encounters) at many tedious company events, helped to explain his gratitude. The wife was a priss. Her name was Cheryl. Her hair looked as if she still used big rollers and embalm-your-hairdo spray. Her mind was room-by-room Laura Ashley wallpaper: tiny, unopened pastel buds arranged in straight rows. She probably put on rubber gloves to make love, and checked it off on a list afterwards. One more messy household chore. She looked at Kat as if she'd like to spritz her with air deodorizer. Kat revenged herself by picturing Cheryl's bathrooms; hand towels embroidered with lilies, fuzzy covers on the toilet seats.

The magazine itself got off to a rocky start. Although Kat had lots of lovely money to play with, and although it was a challenge to be working in colour, she did not have the free hand Gerald had promised her. She had to contend with the company board of directors, who were all men, who were all accountants or indistinguishable from them, who were cautious and slow as moles.

"It's simple," Kat told them. "You bombard them with images of what they ought to be, and you make them feel shitty for being the way they are. You're working with the gap between reality and perception. That's why you have to hit them with something new, something they've never seen before, something they aren't. Nothing sells like anxiety."

The board, on the other hand, felt that their readership should simply be offered more of what they already had. More fur, more sumptuous leather, more cashmere. More established names. The board had no sense of improvisation, no wish to take risks, no sporting instincts, no desire to put one over on the readers just for the hell of it. "Fashion is like hunting," Kat told them, hoping to appeal to their male hormones, if any. "It's playful, it's intense, it's predatory. It's blood and guts. It's erotic." But to them it was about good taste. They wanted Dress-for-Success. Kat wanted scattergun ambush.

Everything became a compromise. Kat had wanted to call the magazine *All the Rage*, but the board was put off by the vibrations of anger in the word "rage." They thought it was too feminist, of all things. "It's a forties sound," Kat said. "Forties is back. Don't you get it?" But they didn't. They wanted to call it *Or*. French for "gold" and blatant enough in its values, but without any base note, as Kat told them. They sawed off at *Felice*, which had qualities each side wanted. It was vaguely French-sounding, it meant "happy" (so much less threatening than "rage"), and, although you couldn't expect the others to notice, for Kat it had a feline bouquet that counteracted the laciness. She had it done in hot pink lipstick-scrawl, which helped some. She could live with it, but it had not been her first love.

This battle has been fought and refought over every innovation in design, every new angle Kat tried to bring in, every innocuous bit of semi-kink. There was a big row over a spread that did lingerie, half pulled off and with broken glass perfume bottles strewn on the floor. There was an uproar over the two nouveau-stockinged legs, one tied to the leg of a chair with a third, different-colored stocking. They had not understood the man's three-hundred-dollar leather gloves positioned ambiguously around a neck.

And so it had gone on, for five years.

After Gerald has left, Kat paces her living room. Pace, pace. Her stitches pull. She's not looking forward to her solitary dinner of microwaved leftovers. She's not sure now why she came back here, to this flat burg beside the polluted inland sea. Was it Ger? Ludicrous thought, but no longer out of the question. Is he the reason she stays, despite her growing impatience with him?

He's no longer fully rewarding. They've learned each other too well, they take shortcuts now; their time together has shrunk from whole stolen, rolling, and sensuous afternoons to a few hours snatched between work and dinnertime. She no longer knows what she wants from him. She tells herself she's worth more, she should branch out; but she doesn't see other men, she can't, somehow. She's tried once or twice, but it didn't work. Sometimes she goes out to dinner or a flick with one of the gay designers. She likes the gossip.

Maybe she misses London. She feels caged, in this country, in this city, in this room. She could start with the room, she could open a window. It's too stuffy in here. There's an undertone of formaldehyde, from Hairball's bottle. The flowers she got for the operation are mostly wilted, all except Gerald's from today. Come to think of it, why didn't he send her any at the hospital? Did he forget, or was it a message?

"Hairball," she says, "I wish you could talk. I could have a more intelligent conversation with you than with most of the losers in this turkey farm." Hairball's baby teeth glint in the light; it looks as if it's about to speak.

Kat feels her own forehead. She wonders if she's running a temperature. Something ominous is going on behind her back. There haven't been enough phone calls from the magazine; they've been able to muddle on without her, which is bad news.

Reigning queens should never go on vacation, or have operations' either. Uneasy lies the head. She has a sixth sense about these things, she's been involved in enough palace coups to know the signs, she has sensitive antennae for the footfalls of impending treachery.

The next morning she pulls herself together, downs an espresso from her mini-machine, picks out an aggressive touch-me-if-you-dare suede outfit in armor gray, and drags herself to the office, although she isn't due in till next week. Surprise, surprise. Whispering knots break up in the corridors, greet her with false welcome as she limps past. She settles herself at her minimalist desk, checks her mail. Her head is pounding, her stitches hurt. Ger gets wind of her arrival; he wants to see her A.S.A.P., and not for lunch.

He awaits her in his newly done wheat-on-white office, with the eighteenth-century desk they chose together, the Victorian inkstand, the framed blowups from the magazine, the hands gloved in maroon leather, wrists manacled with pearls, the Hermes scarf twisted into a blindfold, the model's mouth blossoming lusciously beneath it. Some of her best stuff. He's beautifully done up, in a lick-my-neck silk shirt open at the throat, an eat-your-heart-out Italian silk-and-wool loose knit sweater. Oh, cool insouciance. Oh, eyebrow language.

He's a money man who lusted after art, and now he's got some, now he is some. Body art. Her art. She's done her job well; he's finally sexy.

He's smooth as lacquer. "I didn't want to break this to you until next week," he says. He breaks it to her. It's the board of directors. They think she's too bizarre, they think she goes way too far. Nothing he could do about it, although naturally he tried.

Naturally. Betrayal. The monster has turned on its own mad scientist. "I gave you life," she wants to scream at him.

She isn't in good shape. She can hardly stand. She stands, despite his offer of a chair. She sees now what she's wanted, what she's been missing. Gerald IS what she's been missing: the stable, unfashionable, previous, tight-assed Gerald. Not Ger, not the one she's made in her own image. The other one, before he got ruined. The Gerald with a house and a small child and a picture of his wife in a silver frame on his desk. She wants to be in that silver frame. She wants the child. She's been robbed.

"And who is my lucky replacement?" she says. She needs a cigarette, but does not want to reveal her shaking hands.

"Actually, it's me," he says, trying for modesty.

This is too absurd. Gerald couldn't edit a phone book.

"You?" she says faintly. She has the good sense not to laugh.

"I've always wanted to get out of the money end of things here," he says, "into the creative area. I knew you'd understand, since it can't be you at any rate. I knew you'd prefer someone who could, well, sort of build on your foundations." Pompous asshole. She looks at his neck. She longs for him, hates herself for it, and is powerless.

The room wavers. He slides toward her across the wheat-colored broadloom, takes her by the gray suede upper arms. "I'll write you a good reference," he says. "Don't worry about that. Of course, we can still see one another. I'd miss our afternoons."

"Of course," she says. He kisses her, a voluptuous kiss, or it would look like one to a third party, and she lets him. In a pig's ear.

She makes it home in a taxi. The driver is rude to her and gets away with it; she doesn't have the energy. In her mailbox is an engraved invitation: Ger and Cheryl are having a drinks party, tomorrow evening. Postmarked five days ago. Cheryl is behind the times.

Kat undresses, runs a shallow bath. There's not much to drink around here, there's nothing to sniff or smoke. What an oversight; she's stuck with herself. There are other jobs. There are other men, or that's the theory. Still, something's been ripped out of her. How could this have happened—to her? When knives have been slated for backs, she's always done the stabbing. Any headed her way she's seen coming in time, and thwarted. Maybe she's losing her edge.

She stares into the bathroom mirror, assesses her face in the misted glass. A face of the eighties, a mask face, a bottom-line face; push the weak to the wall and grab what you can. But now it's the nineties. Is she out of style, so soon? She's only thirty-five, and she's already losing track of what people ten years younger are thinking. That could be fatal. As times goes by, she'll have to race faster and faster to keep up, and for what? Part of the life she should have had is just a gap, it isn't there, it's nothing. What can be salvaged from it, what can be redone, what can be done at all?

When she climbs out of the tub after her sponge bath, she almost falls. She has a fever, no doubt about it. Inside her something is leaking, or else festering; she can hear it, like a dripping tap. A running sore, a sore from running so hard. She should go to the emergency ward at some hospital, get herself shot up with antibiotics. Instead, she lurches into the living room, takes Hairball down from the mantelpiece in its bottle, places it on the coffee table. She sits cross-legged, listens. Filaments wave. She can hear a kind of buzz, like bees at work.

She'd asked the doctor if it could have started as a child, a fertilized egg that escaped somehow and got into the wrong place. No, said the doctor. Some people thought this kind of tumor was present in seedling form from birth, or before it. It might be the woman's undeveloped twin. What they really were was unknown. They had many kinds of tissue, though. Even brain tissue. Though of course all of these tissues lack structure.

Still, sitting here on the rug looking in at it, she pictures it as a child. It has come out of her, after all. It is flesh of her flesh. Her child with Gerald, her thwarted child, not allowed to grow normally. Her warped child, taking its revenge.

"Hairball," she says. "You're so ugly. Only a mother could love you." She feels sorry for it. She feels loss. Tears run down her face. Crying is not something she does, not normally, not lately.

Hairball speaks to her, without words. It is irreducible—it has the texture of reality, it is not an image. What it tells her is everything she's never wanted to hear about herself. This is new knowledge, dark and precious and necessary. It cuts.

She shakes her head. What are you doing, sitting on the floor and talking to a hairball? You are sick, she tells herself. Take a Tylenol and go to bed.

The next day she feels a little better. Dania from layout calls her and makes dove like, sympathetic coos at her, and wants to drop by during lunch hour to take a look at her aura. Kat tells her to come off it. Dania gets huffy, and says that Kat's losing her job is a price for immoral behaviour in a previous life. Kat tells her to stuff it; anyway, she'd done enough immoral behavior in this life to account for the whole thing. "Why are you so full of hate?" asks Dania. She doesn't say it like a point she's making, she sounds truly baffled.

"I don't know," says Kat. It's a straight answer.

After she hangs up she paces the floor. She's crackling inside, like hot fat under the broiler. What she's thinking about is Cheryl, bustling about her cozy house, preparing for the party. Cheryl fiddles with her freeze-framed hair, positions an overloaded vase of flowers, fusses about the caterers. Gerald comes in, kisses her lightly on the cheek. A connubial scene. His conscience is nicely washed. The witch is dead, his foot is on the body, the trophy; he's had his dirty fling, he's ready now for the rest of his life.

Kat takes a taxi to the David Wood Food Shop and buys two dozen chocolate truffles. She has them put into an oversized box, then into an oversized bag with the store logo on it. Then she goes home and takes Hairball out of its bottle. She drains it in the kitchen strainer and pats it damp-dry, tenderly, with paper towels. She sprinkles it with powdered cocoa, which forms a brown pasty crust. It still smells like formaldehyde, so she wraps it in Saran Wrap and then in tinfoil, and then in pink tissue paper, which she ties with a mauve bow. She places it in the David Wood Box in a bed of shredded tissue, with the truffles nestled around. She closes the box, tapes it, puts it into the bag, stuffs several sheets of pink paper on top. It's her gift, valuable and dangerous. It's her messenger, but the message it will deliver is its own. It will tell the truth to whoever asks. It's right that Gerald should have it; after all, it's his child, too.

She prints on the card, "Gerald, Sorry I couldn't be with you. This is all the rage. Love, K."

When evening has fallen and the party must be in full swing, she calls a delivery taxi. Cheryl will not distrust anything that arrives in such an expensive bag. She will open it in public, in front of everyone. There will be distress, there will be questions. Secrets will be unearthed. There will be pain. After that, everything will go way too far.

She is not well; her heart is pounding, space is wavering once more. But outside the window it's snowing—the soft, damp, windless flakes of her child-hood. She puts on her coat and goes out, foolishly. She intends to walk just to the corner, but when she reaches the corner she goes on. The snow melts against her face like small fingers touching. She has done an outrageous thing, but she doesn't feel guilty. She feels light and peaceful and filled with charity, and temporarily without a name.

DARRYL WHETTER

## THE EXTINCTION

of female pubic hair
was never Tim Berners-Lee's intention.
we clicked our way
into his Web then abandoned
the bouquet of that churning tuft.
inky black, chestnut brown, the blonde
of Scandinavia or strawberries, the ginger
husk now as rare as MC1R, that chromosomal
splash of red

not just photogenic
gender camp alopecia
or the new low
in the slutty arms race,
this decade's tramp-stamp tattoo,
the will she or won't she,
but brokered self-delight

doubly naked, even young renters
can enjoy a home-owner's pride,
rolling up the carpet, exposing the fresh
grain of the sanded floor.
meet the market-day grin
of a poulterer with pungent thumbs.
before the hidden itch
of this hidden itch

folds of softest kid
the smiling, daily obscenity
of her pleated velour.

that stretched, sans-serif M
mantra, moan
mmm-hmmm

less
so very much
more

## WINTER HEAT

You and I. We
Warm the cabin
With a fiesta.
Slow dances.
Torturous torch songs.

I favour kiosk chocolate,
Cormorants black as cinder.
He who orchestrates touch,
Who once handed me
My limping orders,
Favours things melted.

You ban air quotes and kink.
Me, fake railings and balloon releases,
Especially for no occasion.
You inform me that yes
Some gingers are cold.
I confide that meanly handsome
Hot-headed micks
Only made me think of we.

# EDITORS

## CLARK, Kim

Kim Clark is a Nanaimo author, poet and playwright. Clark has published short fiction—*Attemptations* (Caitlin Press 2012)—and poetry—*Middle Child of Summer* (Leaf Press 2014), *Sit You Waiting* (Caitlin Press 2013) and *Dis ease ad De sire, the M anu S cript* (Lipstick Press 2012). She's been a finalist in Theatre BC's Playwrights Competition, has a novella optioned for a feature-length film and her darkly comic *A One-Handed Novel* arrives in 2017 via Caitlin Press.

Kim's hair has morphed from penny-bright to rich auburn and is now threatened with silver.

## KRESAN, Dawn Marie

Dawn Marie Kresan is an author, editor and graphic designer. Her books include the limited-edition chapbook *Framed* (2009), and the full-length poetry collection *Muse* (Tightrope Books 2013). She also co-edited, with Susan Holbrook, *Detours: an anthology of poets from Windsor & Essex County* (Palimpsest Press 2013). Kresan was on the 2016 shortlist for the CBC Poetry Prize. Her nonfiction work *Derelict* is forthcoming (Biblioasis 2018).

Dawn's hair was a coppery strawberry blonde much of her life, and she hated it, trying to bleach it with Sun-In and lemons. Now middle aged, her red hair has naturally faded, and she frequently washes it in pigment enhancing shampoos to recreate the hair she once had.

# CONTRIBUTORS

## ATWOOD, Margaret

Margaret Atwood is the author of more than forty books of fiction, poetry, and critical essays. Her novels include *The Blind Assassin*, winner of the Booker Prize; *Alias Grace*, which won the Giller Prize in Canada and the Premio Mondello in Italy; and *The Handmaid's Tale,* which is now a TV series with Hulu. Her most recent books include *Hag-Seed* (2016), a novel revisitation of Shakespeare's play *The Tempest*, and *Angel Catbird,* a graphic novel with co-creator Johnnie Christmas. Margaret Atwood lives in Toronto with writer Graeme Gibson.

Margaret describes her hair as being a reddish dead-fox colour until it went white.

## CHAFE, Aidan

Aidan Chafe is author of the poetry chapbooks *Sharpest Tooth* (Anstruther Press 2016) and *Right Hand Hymns* (Frog Hollow Press 2017). His poetry has appeared in *Cordite Poetry Review*, *CV2* and *Scrivener Creative Review*. By day he works as a public-school teacher and by night he works as an active board member for the Royal City Literary Arts Society in New Westminster.

It's fitting that Aidan turned out a redhead. His mother's a Dubliner and in Gaelic the meaning of the name Aidan is "Little Fire."

## CLINK, Carolyn

Carolyn Clink won the 2011 Aurora Award for Best Poem/Song for "The ABCs of the End of the World." She's a member of the Algonquin Square Table poetry workshop in Toronto and the Science Fiction Poetry Association. Her Canadian poetry publications include: *Chiaroscuro, White Wall Review, Imaginarium 2012: The Best Canadian Speculative Writing, Hart House Review, On-Spec, Tesseracts, Gusts: Contemporary Tanka, Room*, and *The Dalhousie Review*.

Carolyn moved from strawberry blonde as a child to tri-coloured hair (red, blonde and brown) and now to quadri-coloured hair (if you consider white to be a colour).

## DOLMAN, Anita

Anita Dolman's poetry and short fiction have been published throughout Canada and the United States. Her poetry recently appeared in *Matrix Magazine, Ottawater* and *Bywords*. Her fiction recently appeared in *Matrix Magazine*, the anthology *Triangulation: Lost Voices* (Parsec Ink 2015) and *On Spec Magazine*. She is the author of two poetry chapbooks, *Where No One Can See You* (AngelHousePress 2014) and *Scalpel, tea and shot glass* (above/ground press 2004), and was a finalist for the 2015 Alberta Magazine Award for fiction. Dolman is a contributing editor for *Arc Poetry Magazine*.

Anita's son, father and siblings are all vividly redheads, but she, herself, is a former drugstore calico, now slowly learning to make peace with her white and blonde.

## FOSS, Maureen

Maureen Foss lives in the heart of the Cariboo with her husband, Gary, and assorted pets. She has four published novels, *The Cadillac Kind (Polestar 1996), Rat Trap Murders (Nightwood Editions 2000), Scribes (Caitlin Press 2011)* and due out Fall 2018, *Sleeping With Strangers* (Oolichan Books). She has been a member of an established writing group for thirty years. A hunter-gatherer, she constructs baskets and wreaths from found treasures. Her big vegetable gardens feed the family.

Maureen inherited her red hair, called a strawberry-blonde, from her dad. His bushy red eyebrows were intersected with scars from playing lacrosse. Maureen's pretty much like him in walk, temperament and attitude, without the scars.

## FRASER, David

David Fraser is a poet, spoken-word performer, publisher and editor. He lives in Nanoose Bay on Vancouver Island. His poetry has appeared in many journals and anthologies, including *Rocksalt, An Anthology of Contemporary BC Poetry* (Mother Tongue Press 2008), *Walk Myself Home* (Caitlin Press 2010), *Poems from Planet Earth* (Leaf Press 2013) and recently *Tesseracts 18*. He has published six collections of poetry. His most recent collection is *After All the Scissor Work is Done* (Leaf Press 2016).

David's a strawberry blond. "Every year, I arrive at the hockey dressing room to meet the new coach. He looks at me, says, "How you doing, Red?"

## GOLDBERG, Kim

Kim Goldberg is the author of seven books of poetry and nonfiction including *Undetectable*, a haibun diary of her Hepatitis C journey, and *Red Zone*, poems of urban homelessness. She is a winner of the Rannu Fund Poetry Prize for Speculative Literature. Her reality-bending poems and tales have appeared in the *Tesseracts* anthologies, *Imaginarium 2015, Dark Mountain, Literary Review of Canada, Geist* and elsewhere. She lives and speculates in Nanaimo, BC, and online at https://pigsquash.wordpress.com/.

Kim loves her auburn hair, her autumnal hair, her burning, burnished hair of harvest leaves, her coat of many colours, her coat of long sleeves that shall never be cut short.

## HALEY, Heather

Trailblazing poet, Heather Haley, pushes boundaries by creatively integrating disciplines, genres and media. Her writing has appeared in *Geist*, the *Antigonish Review*, *FORCE Field: Women Poets of British Columbia* and *The Revolving City*. Haley was an editor for the *LA Weekly* and publisher of the *Edgewise Cafe*, one of Canada's first electronic literary magazines. She is the author of poetry collections *Sideways* (Anvil Press 2003) and *Three Blocks West of Wonderland* (Ekstasis Editions 2009), and debut novel, *The Town Slut's Daughter* (Howe Sound Publishing 2014). Check out her website: www.heatherhaley.com.

Heather and her red hair have been described as "fiery," though she often feels shy and hides behind it like a veil.

## HAMON, Tracy

Tracy Hamon was born in Regina, Saskatchewan. She holds an MA in English from the University of Regina. Her first book of poetry *This Is Not Eden* was released in April 2005 and was a finalist for two Saskatchewan Book Awards. *Interruptions in Glass* won the 2005 City of Regina Writing Award and was shortlisted for two Saskatchewan Book Awards in 2010. Her third collection *Red Curls* won the Drs. Morris and Jacqui Shumiatcher Regina Book Award in 2015.

Tracy describes her hair as "Tiger two-toned."

## HARTSFIELD, Carla

Carla Hartsfield is a poet, singer/songwriter, pianist and guitar player. Her most recent full-length album, *Just Once Forever*, was launched at the Cadillac Lounge in December 2016. Her poetry books include *Your Last Day on Earth* (Brick Books 2004), and *Little Hearts* (Rubicon Press 2016).

Carla's hair is auburn. Her grandmother used to say it was the colour of a copper penny.

## KEMP, Penn

A performance poet, activist and playwright, Penn Kemp is London, Ontario's inaugural Poet Laureate and the League of Canadian Poets Spoken Word Artist of 2015. As Western University's Writer-in-Residence, her project was the DVD, *Luminous*

*Entrance: a Sound Opera for Climate Change Action*. Her latest work includes editing two anthologies, *Performing Women* and *Women and Multimedia* (www.poets.ca/feministcaucus), and new poetry, *Barbaric Cultural Practice*. Her play, *The Triumph of Teresa Harris*, is being produced in 2017.

Penn's hair has gone from strawberry blonde as a child to copper as a girl and auburn as a woman. Now she's pinto/pied in half: the top of her head is grey, but the back she identifies with is still reddish-brown.

## LANTHIER, KATERI

Kateri Lanthier's poems have appeared in journals in Canada, the U.S. and England, most recently in *Green Mountains Review, The Fiddlehead, Hazlitt, Arc, Event* and The *Literary Review of Canada*. Her first collection is *Reporting from Night* (Iguana 2011). She won the 2013 Walrus Poetry Prize and third prize in the 2016 Troubadour International Poetry contest. *Siren*, her second collection, will be published by Signal Editions, Véhicule Press in 2017.

Kateri's hair is October amber-burnt ruby. Red hair: her childhood roots rediscovered, her adult indulgence.

## LEVY, JOANNE

A survivor of the corporate world, Joanne Levy now works from home, supporting other authors and writing for kids, creating the friends she wishes she had when she was a tween. She lives in Southern Ontario with her husband, cats, a mean African Grey parrot, and a sweet but not-so-smart dog. Joanne's published novels for children include *Crushing It* (Aladdin 2017) and *Small Medium at Large* (Bloomsbury USA 2012).

Raised as the only redhead in a family of brunettes, Joanne, once known to hate her unique locks, now embraces her gingerness in all its freckly, fiery glory.

## LINN, WINONA

Winona Linn is an award-winning artist and poet who has performed her poetry all over the world. Currently, she lives in Paris, France, where she is the director of Paris Lit Up's Slam Project, and is working on her fourth book, a graphic novel.

Winona's red hair and green dresses make her look like an immature strawberry, and she has no problem with this.

## LOWTHER, Christine

Christine Lowther's book, *Born Out of This* (Caitlin Press 2014), was shortlisted for the Roderick Haig-Brown Regional category of the BC Book Prizes. She later served as a judge for that prize. Chris won the CNF category in the 2015 Federation of British Columbia Writers' Literary Writes. She was presented with the inaugural Pacific Rim Arts Society Rainy Coast Arts Award for Significant Accomplishment in 2014. She has written three books of poetry and co-edited two anthologies.

Christine was born with copper hair and freckles and saw it as a curse at the time.

## MEYER, Bruce

Bruce Meyer is author of 50 books of poetry, short-fiction, and non-fiction including the award-winning *The Seasons* (Porcupine's Quill 2014), *The Arrow of Time* (Ronsdale Press 2015), *The Madness of Planets* (Black Moss Press 2015), and *To Linares* (2016). His book *Portraits of Canadian Writers* (Porcupine's Quill 2016) was recently a national bestseller. He lives in Barrie and teaches at Georgian College and Victoria College at the University of Toronto.

Bruce's mother told him his hair was on fire, and that he had the temperament to match it.

## PĂPUCARU, Rebecca

Rebecca Păpucaru's poetry has appeared in *ARC*, *The Malahat Review*, *The New Quarterly*, *The Literary Review of Canada*, *EVENT*, *Prism international*, and *The Antigonish Review*, among others. She was shortlisted for the Penguin Random House Canada Student Award for Fiction. Anthologies include *I Found It at the Movies: An Anthology of Film Poems* (Guernica Editions 2014), and *The Best Canadian Poetry in English* (Tightrope Books 2010). She is editing a poetry manuscript, *The Panic Room*.

Rebecca's natural hair colour is auburn (apologies to the true gingers) which she tints dark brown to avoid "brassiness". If she doesn't, she's falsely accused of dyeing her hair red, the brassy truth being less credible than fiction, however deep and even its tone.

## PETCH, Charlie

Cathy Charlie Petch is an auburn-toned playwright, spoken-word artist, haiku deathmaster and musical saw player. Their full collection *Late Night Knife Fights* was published with Lyrical Myrical Press. They have been published by *Descant*, *The Toronto Quarterly* and*a*. Petch is a member of The League of Canadian Poets and is the creative director of "Hot Damn It's a Queer Slam". They are happiest onstage. Find out more at www.charliecpetch.com

Charlie Petch prefers to appear as if their brain is a 5-alarm fire.

## PRESTON, Rachael

Rachael Preston is the author of three novels. Goose Lane Editions published *Tent of Blue* (2002) and *The Wind Seller* (2006), which won the City of Hamilton Arts Award. *The Fishers of Paradise* (Wolsak & Wynn 2016) won the Arts Hamilton inaugural Kerry Schooley Award. In 2016 *The Fishers of Paradise* became the 16th Bookmark on Project Bookmark Canada's literary trail when a plaque was unveiled on Hamilton's Desjardins Trail. Rachael lives and writes lives in Nanaimo, BC.

I had forgotten my mother was a redhead until I happened on an old photograph and found myself transfixed, trying to reconcile that rich vivid colour, that knockout redness, with my idea of who we both were.

## SPEARS, Heather

Heather Spears, Vancouver-born writer and artist, has lived in Denmark since 1962. Her books: 14 collections of poetry, five novels, and 4 books of drawings. Major awards: Governor-General's Award and CBC Literary Award, 3x Pat Lowther Award. Heather instructs drawing, writes about drawing and the brain in *The Creative Eye* (2007, 2012) and specializes in drawing premature infants. Heather draws in theatres, concert halls, courtrooms, hospitals and war zones. She has held over 80 solo exhibitions in Europe and America. www.heatherspears.com

Heather describes her relationship to red hair as once bright red, now faded and sparse.

## TUCKER, Diane

Vancouver native, Diane Tucker, has published three poetry books—*God on His Haunches* (Nightwood Editions 1996), *Bright Scarves of Hours* (Palimpsest Press 2007), *Bonsai Love* (Harbour Publishing 2014)—and a YA novel, *His Sweet Favour* (Thistledown Press 2009). Her first full-length play, *Here Breaks the Heart: The Loves of Christina Rossetti*, was produced by Fire Exit Theatre in Calgary in 2013. Her most recent poetry manuscript, *The Five Seasons*, is looking for its publishing home.

When Diane was young, they said her hair was strawberry blond. These days the nice people at L'Oreal call it Copper Blonde—red like a penny. It occurs to her that someday she'll have to explain to her grandchildren what a penny was.

## VIOLET, Lizzie

Writer and Spoken Word artist, Lizzie Violet, is known for dark themes in her poetry, prose and storytelling. Lizzie has been performing her Spoken Word on stages across Toronto for many years, featuring at Wordspell, Livewords, Pride, Plasticine, Artbar and Nuit Blanche. In 2015 she won The Best Original Poet and runner-up prize for Best Spoken Word Artist in *Now Magazine* readers' poll. Lizzie also performs in The Redhead Revue with Heather Babcock. www.lizzieviolet.com

Lizzie's hellfire red hair gives her the bold brave determination to perform superhero acts that the adrenaline rush of coffee just can't reach.

## WATKINS, Jordan Lloyd

Jordan Lloyd Watkins is a multidisciplinary artist whose body of work includes theatre, dance, live art and film. He is most interested in pursuing dynamic storytelling—work that is accessible, engaging and relevant. As a creator, he considers the evolution of technology as his way into qualifying contemporary values, lifestyle, and social order. He is also the creative director of Truer Titles, a completely untrustworthy source for satirical news.

Jordan says, "Having the red scourge has made me as close to perfection as humanly possible. Humble, too."

## WHETTER, Darryl

Darryl Whetter's five books include the pot-smuggling novel, *Keeping Things Whole* (Vagrant Press 2013), and the bicycle odyssey, *The Push & the Pull* (Goose Lane Editions 2008). His debut collection of stories was a *Globe and Mail* Top 100 Book. A professor of creative writing, he reviews books regularly for papers such as *The Globe and Mail* and *The National Post*. The poem here is taken from *Search Box Bed*, his 2017 collection devoted to networked sexuality. www.darrylwhetter.ca

Of auburn beard and once-dark hair, Darryl has never forgotten a folklore dictionary's warning about "never trusting a man with a red beard and black hair." His carrot-top niece was recently the flower girl at his wedding.

## ZILM, Jennifer

Jennifer Zilm is a former biblical scholar, community mental health work, librarian and almost archivist. She is the author of *Waiting Room* (BookThug 2016) and two chapbooks, *October Notebook* (Dancing Girl Press 2015) and *The Whole and Broken Yellows* (Frog Hollow 2013). A forthcoming collection will be published by Guernica Editions in 2018. Her work has appeared in journals across Canada.

Jennifer was a strawberry blonde and became full-stop red after puberty. She avoids the sun and has realized that the only desert she will live in is the one in her mind.

## ACKNOWLEDGEMENTS

We thank the following presses and authors for their permission to reprint their work:

PAGE 47: "For the Daughters of Chernobyl" by Rebecca Păpucaru first appeared in *SLAB: Sound and Literary Artbook* (Slippery Rock University, Vol.6. 2011).

PAGES 50-56: "'Nobody ever did want me'" was previously published as "Afterword" by Margaret Atwood in *Anne of Green Gables* (New Canadian Library, 1992). Afterword copyright © 1992, O. W. Toad Ltd. Used with permission of the author.

PAGES 82-93: "Hairball" was previously published in *Wilderness Tips* by Margaret Atwood. Copyright © 1991, O.W. Toad, Ltd. Reprinted by permission of Emblem/McClelland & Stewart, a division of Penguin Random House Canada Limited.

PAGE 94: "The Extinction" by Darryl Whetter was previously published in *Search Box Bed* (Palimpsest Press, 2017). Copyright © 2017, reprinted by permission of the publisher.